THE MINISTRY OF HELPS HANDBOOK

HOW TO BE TOTALLY EFFECTIVE SERVING IN THE MINISTRY OF HELPS

by Dr. Buddy Bell

Harrison House
Tulsa, Oklahoma

23 22 21   12 11 10

The Ministry of Helps Handbook—
How To Be Totally Effective Serving in the Ministry of Helps
ISBN-13: 978-1-60683-007-9
Copyright © 1990 by Buddy Bell
Revised Edition 2009
Tulsa, Oklahoma

Published by Harrison House Publishers
Tulsa, Oklahoma 74145

CONTENTS

FOREWORD

When Buddy Bell says he is a "pastor's friend," he really is. When we first had Buddy minister in our church, we more than doubled our volunteer work staff. He helps people understand that their call to the helps ministry in the local church is vital and fulfilling. It blesses a pastor's heart to see people doing life together and everyone serving with joy in this community called the *local church*. I believe this book is Buddy's best yet. His passion is clear through each story and each chapter for every believer not to tolerate church, but to really enjoy it and be a vital part of what God is doing today.

Pastor Robert Barriger
Camino de Vida
Lima, Peru
www.lifemissions.com

*   *   *

My greatest challenge as a pastor is motivating people in the church to help with the many behind-the-scenes tasks. In reading Rev. Bell's new book, *The Ministry of Helps Handbook,* I found the answer. It is the most practical and inspiring book on the subject that I have read, and I will be using it in our new members' class for years to come.

Mike Buie
Cathedral of Praise
Sand Springs, Oklahoma

The ministry of helps is the most overlooked, underrated ministry in the church. Every year thousands of pastors leave the ministry. Most pastors quit because they are over worked and burned out. With a healthy ministry of helps at their disposal, this number would be considerably lower. Buddy Bell shares proven biblical principles that will help equip the local church to fulfill its God-given mandate while enjoying the experience. This book is a must-read for leaders and lay people alike.

Dr. Jim Willoughby
Senior Pastor
Echos of Faith World Outreach Ministries
Ontario, CA

*   *   *

You hold in your hands the road map to an exciting future!

Buddy Bell is a travel agent who has helped to send tens of thousands of people on a journey to a place far beyond the mundane. He will lead the way past the boundaries of just going through the motions. Pack your bags and get ready for the adventure of a lifetime.

Countless churches have been transformed into launching pads for significant, life-changing ministry through the leadership of Buddy Bell. On these pages you will begin to understand that you are a major key for your church to experience the greater things God wants to do.

Thank the Lord for pastors and church leaders, but the transformation begins when every child of God begins to discover their place of service and ministry.

I am thrilled that you are taking this step and moving beyond the past. Your journey begins today! Read each word prayerfully and embrace the dream that God places in your heart.

B. G. Nevitt
Senior Pastor
Decatur, Illinois
www.gtChurch.com

Buddy and Kathy Bell have been a tremendous blessing to Omega Church for many years. *The Ministry of Helps Handbook*, is an even greater blessing. Just when we think that Buddy has done his best, he causes us to believe even more that the ministry of helps is the greatest ministry of all.

Pastors Ronnie and Zona Allen
Senior Pastors
Omega Church
San Antonio, TX

*   *   *

Rev. Buddy Bell is a trailblazing pioneer in the ministry of helps. He is a man who has brought great encouragement and purpose to the lives of multitudes of believers called to serve in this often unrecognized, but vitally important, ministry. He is truly a "pastor's friend" who understands the importance of "every joint supplies." This book is full of insights on the importance of the ministry of helps in the local church. It showcases biblical examples of those who served as ministers of help, and it is a delightful read marked with Rev. Bell's trademark humor.

get caught and never get out.

There are not two rooms in the Church! There is only one. There is not a division in the body of Christ. There is only one Body. There are no "big guns and little guns" but one "gun," the body of Christ.

IS THE MINISTRY OF HELPS BIBLICAL?

When they first begin to hear about a ministry of helps, some people wonder if that is in the Bible.

One brother said, "You know, if there is any new-fangled doctrine, it comes out of Tulsa, Oklahoma."

Christians today want to know that they are really part of the church. They want to be participants, not spectators. When they are involved in the ministry of helps, they will *know* they are active participants.

Look at the Apostle Paul's first letter to the church at Corinth.

> **And God hath set some in the church, first apostles, secondarily prophets, thirdly teachers, after that miracles, then gifts of healings, *helps*, governments, diversities of tongues.**
>
> **1 Corinthians 12:28**

Right there in the Word of God it says *helps*. No man made it up. No committee put it into the church. This is not a "new-fangled doctrine" out of Tulsa.

The word *help(s)* is the Greek word *antilepsis* or *antilempsis*, which means "a laying hold of, an exchange," or "to lay hold of, so as to support."[1]

In other words, if you are helping anyone in the church, or if you are helping the weak or needy, you are operating in the ministry of helps, a "gift" set in the church by God. This is a ministry just as valid, just as anointed, as if God had asked you to be a prophet. God is not a respecter of persons, nor should we be.

An usher, a nursery worker, a soundman, a musician—anyone giving assistance in the body—is in the ministry of helps.

Their tasks are just as important as those of people in leadership offices. God's rewards are not based on the size of the ministry on earth but on the degree of faithfulness. Using the crowbar of faithfulness will bring you as many rewards in heaven for sweeping floors—if that is where God put you—as it will for building the biggest church in the country.

FAITHFULNESS MAKES THE DIFFERENCE

Faithfulness is necessary to everyone in the helps ministries. Take nursery workers: The first thing many parents say when they come to pick up their children is, "Boy, did we have a great service. You really missed it!" To some, the nursery room is the "missed-it" room.

---

[1] W. E. Vine, *Vine's Expository Dictionary of Old and New Testament Words* (Old Tappan: Fleminging H. Revell Company, 1981), Volume 2, p. 213.

school bus. The ride home took about an hour, so I sat up close to the front and watched the bus driver shift those gears and pump that clutch. I knew that in about an hour I'd be doing the same thing.

At long last I got home, got off the school bus, and hopped on my bicycle. My grandfather's farm was about a mile and a half away, and while I was riding my bicycle over there, all I could think about was driving that truck and how I was going to shift those gears and pump that clutch.

When I reached my grandfather's farm, I went directly into the barn, but my heart sank when I saw the truck. It was sitting by the tool shop with its hood up, and I thought, *Something's wrong.* I walked into the shop, and Grandpa was there. He had the carburetor out of the truck, and it was all torn apart on the workbench.

I looked at him and said, "Grandpa, what are you doing?"

He said, "Well, Buddy, the truck wasn't running too well so I stopped, took the carburetor off, and took it apart to clean it. I'm going to put it back together here in just a little bit, and we'll get it going again."

"Hurry up, Grandpa!" I said. I'd been waiting all day to drive that truck.

Grandpa cleaned the different parts of the carburetor, and then he began to put it back together. I noticed that he was taking more time with the smaller parts than he was with the bigger parts. On many of the little parts, he would go over to the shelf, get a book, and read about them for a few minutes before he would work on them.

That was just too much for me to bear. I soon blurted out, "Grandpa! Don't mess with the little parts. Just put the big parts together. I want to drive the truck right now."

"Oh no, Buddy," he said. "We've got to have all the parts, big and small, to this carburetor and we've got to have them all adjusted properly, or this truck won't run right. It'll run, but we won't get the full potential, the full power out of this engine."

"I don't care about all that," I said. "Just put the thing together, Grandpa, and let me drive. That's all I want to do right now."

He stood there for a moment with a thoughtful look on his face. Then he said, "Buddy, I want to prove something to you. You think some of these little parts are not that important, so I'm going to put the carburetor together and leave out some of them. I'm going to prove to you how important they really are."

My grandfather proceeded to put the smaller parts on the workbench. He then put the big parts of the carburetor together and put it back in the truck. Then he got in and fired it up. The engine took off for a few seconds, but then it flooded out. Grandpa turned to me and said, "Now, Buddy, the reason this is happening is because you think that these so-called little parts are not that important, so I've left them out. But that's why the truck is not running properly.

God hath set some in the church, first apostles, secondarily prophets, thirdly teachers, after that, miracles, then gifts of healings, *helps*, governments, diversities of tongues.

1 Corinthians 12:28

This is what God wants in the church. You would be amazed at how many times I've been asked if the ministry of helps is in the Bible, but there it is.

People are wide-eyed when they start to study this verse. They love to read about having apostles, prophets, teachers, working of miracles, gifts of healings—the ministry gifts that sound exciting—in the church. But these same people blink right over *helps*. They think, *What's that doing in the midst of all those exciting things for God?*

The truth is that God set the ministry of helps in the church. No man made it up. No committee put it together. It says right there in 1 Corinthians 12:28 that the same God who created the heavens and the earth set the ministry of helps in the church.

Over twenty-five years ago I discovered the ministry of helps. I saw that it is a supernatural ministry that is just as valid and just as anointed as the offices of a preacher or a prophet. The reason is that our God is not a respecter of people. (Acts 10:34.) In other words, He does not value some of us above others.

We have what I call "specialties" for God. These are particular callings or giftings that each individual believer can give Him to use to fulfill His purpose: the salvation of the world. (John 3:16.)

12

Wherever we fit in the body, we are of equal value in God's eyes.

What has happened to the church? Why do we respect some in the body of Christ and regard them as higher than we do others? Doesn't the Bible say that we are all in this thing together?

Please understand my heart. I'm not saying this to take anything away from prophets or apostles or any of the other ministry gifts. I thank God for all of them. I just believe that we should be what God wants each of us to be because the church needs every member. We need all the parts of the body working together.

How effective can the church be if we are all doing our part? When the disciples got their ministry of helps together, Acts 6:7-8 says, "The Word of God increased...the number of the disciples multiplied in Jerusalem greatly," and "great wonders and miracles" were done "among the people." Sounds like they began to change their world! That is how effective we can be if all members of the body—big and small—will understand their importance and do their part with passion and excellence.

EXCITED TO SERVE

To be in the ministry of helps is to be "usefully employed in various ways as aids in promoting the temporal or spiritual welfare of the church."[1] Noah Webster defines the word *helps* as

---

[1] Albert Barnes, DD., *Barnes' Notes*, Electronic Database (Copyright ©1977 by Biblesoft), "1 Corinthians 12:28."

Some of the most destroying, negative words are spoken after church services by church members to nursery workers in hundreds of churches throughout this country. Then we wonder why the pastor has such a hard time getting people to serve outside of the sanctuary. One reason is that people who serve there are constantly being told that they missed God.

How can you miss God when you're serving Him? I think the only way you can miss God is when you're sitting around, doing nothing. We have no shortage of those people in our churches!

In my case, for five and a half years I searched, trying to find my place in the body of Christ. I would come to church and think, *There's got to be more than driving to a building, sitting in a room, listening to stories about God, and going home. There's got to be more.*

I'll be honest with you. I thought, *If this is it, forget it!* Eventually I ran off to a Bible school, trying to be the man of the hour, the man of faith and power in the pulpit. It didn't take long before I found out that it wasn't for me.

Then my wife and I got involved in a church where the pastor believed in raising up an army, not just an audience. I didn't realize it at the time, but it's easier to raise up an audience than it is an army. All the pastor has to do is tickle them behind the ear, where it feels good, with a nice sermon. But when you raise up an army, the toes are going to hurt because they're marching for the Lord and they're being stepped on a lot.

After a couple of months in that church, I said, "Kathy, there really is more to church than just driving to a building, sitting in a room, listening to stories about God, and going home." Funny thing was, every time we turned around we were called *weird*, *strange*, or *different*.

People would point at us, laugh out loud, and say, "God broke the mold when He made you two," just because Kathy and I were at the church every time the doors opened. We served in the nursery together. We would come on Saturday nights and clean the church to get it ready for Sunday mornings. And we didn't say we had to pray about it whenever we were asked to do something. Those words have never come out of our mouths. Whenever we've been asked to serve God, we would say *yes*.

I believe that when your pastor asks you to do something in the church and you tell him that you have to pray about it, you're actually telling him that you hear from God, but he doesn't. Now either your pastor hears from God or he doesn't hear from God. If you don't think he hears from God, you need to go find one who does and attend his church.

Sometimes I'd go home from church at night and actually cry because of the things people called me. My pastor would tell me that it's just how some Christians react to someone who serves in church because they don't understand why we do the work that we do. That made sense, but it didn't make me feel better.

I'll never forget the Sunday morning that I sat in church, and my pastor at that time opened up to 1 Corinthians 12:28 and began to read it out loud. When he got to that little word *helps*, he stopped. For a few minutes he talked about the ministry of helps. He did not preach or teach a message on the ministry of helps as I'm doing in this book, but he *expounded* on the ministry of helps. I had never heard it or seen it in the Bible before, and I'll never forget that moment.

I sat there with tears in my eyes, and I thought, *I'm not weird. I'm not strange. I'm not different. Most of all, God didn't break the mold when He made me. The mold is still in the Bible.*

Finally, after searching for five and a half years—confused, frustrated, and many times very angry toward God—I found out there was nothing wrong with me when I got excited during the offering because I was one of the ushers who got to hand out the envelopes and pass the bucket, because I wanted to come in on Saturday nights and clean the church and get it ready for everybody else on Sunday mornings, or because I wanted to go back into the nursery with my wife and serve so another family could hear the Word of God in the sanctuary.

I found out that morning that I had a ministry, and that it was called the ministry of helps. That's why every time I read the definition by Rev. Godbey, it just goes off on the inside of me like fireworks. It's me, and it's many other believers in the church today. It may even be you!

Do you understand now why God led you to read this book? I believe that this message is for you to help you find your place in the church (Eph. 2:10 NIV), or to remind you why you do what you do if you've already found your place.

God created His plan for the church in advance—and your part in it. As you read on, you're going to see some familiar believers who made it possible for one Man to fulfill His goal and change the world through His ministry because they found their place in the body of Christ.

STUDY NOTES

Divine Design

1. What did the author learn about the body of Christ when his grandfather was fixing the carburetor on his truck?

2. The story of the carburetor is an illustration of what?

Divine Setup

3. Read 1 Corinthians 12:27. How do you personally relate to the statement that you are a member "in particular" in the body of Christ?

4. Read 1 Corinthians 12:28. What does this say about the ministry of helps?

5. What does 1 Corinthians 12:27-28 say about God's attitude toward the body of Christ?

6. What can happen when every member of the body does his or her part?

Excited To Serve

7. In your own words, define the ministry of helps.

8. Has the Holy Spirit ever prompted you to operate in the ministry of helps? How did you respond? Did you feel "led"?

9. Why do you think Reverend Godbey was so excited about the ministry of helps?

10. What has been your attitude toward nursery workers, ushers, and other helps ministers in the past? What is your attitude now?

Watch Your Words

11. When are some of the most destroying words spoken?

12. What is the only way you can miss God?

13. What is the difference between an audience and an army?

3

ELISHA, THE MAN OF GOD

Before we can understand Elisha and the "crowbar of God," we will have to get a good look at the man he followed — Elijah. He is first mentioned in 1 Kings 17.

Elijah, the Tishbite, the prophet of God, appeared on the scene with the declaration that there would be no more rain, not even dew on the ground, until he said so. That is exactly what happened.

As you read the story of Elijah, you will find that during the ensuing drought, he remained for a time by the brook of Cherith. There ravens brought him meat and bread each morning and evening until the brook dried up.

Later, Elijah was sent by God to a widow's house in a town in Zidon, totally out of Israelite territory. He told the widow that if she gave him the last of her food, she would not run out of food again. She obeyed, and the prophet's words came true. When her only son died, Elijah raised him from the dead. Are you beginning to see what sort of man Elisha followed?

About three years later, Elijah challenged the prophets of Baal to prove whose god was God. (1 Kings 18.) The God who consumed the sacrifice by fire would be acknowledged to be the true God, and all would follow Him.

Before he challenged the prophets of Baal, he challenged the people. Men of God always challenge the people of God before they deal with things of Satan or with the world. Elijah said:

> **And Elijah came unto all the people, and said, How long halt ye between two opinions? if the Lord be God, follow him: but if Baal, then follow him. And the people answered him not a word.**
>
> **1 Kings 18:21**

You cannot get any plainer than that. The people did not answer Elijah. They did not say a word (there was no commitment) — until after they saw signs and wonders. When they did not answer, Elijah pointed out that he was the only prophet remaining of the true God (a little later, however, the Lord told him there actually were 7,000 people in Israel who had not bowed their knees to Baal). But at the time, Elijah really believed he was the only one left. He was ready to stand against 450 false prophets because he knew whose God was real.

SHOWDOWN AT HIGH NOON

The 450 prophets of Baal built their altar, placed their sacrifice on it, and began to cry out to their gods. They cried out and cried out. They cut themselves with knives to draw blood for their gods. But no matter how much time Elijah gave them, no fire came down from heaven to consume the sacrifice.

At noon, the Bible says, Elijah began to mock them.

"What's the matter, guys? Is he asleep? Perhaps he has gone on vacation. Yell a little louder, guys!"

I would not have been surprised if old Elijah was rolling on the ground laughing. Would you be too nervous to mock the prophets of Baal? It is all right to laugh at the devil, but you don't want to laugh at him too much, right? There is no telling what he might do, right? No. Elijah knew the Lord whom he served.

After the prophets of Baal did all they could to bring down fire, Elijah took over. He rebuilt the altar, placed his sacrifice on it, and then called for four barrels of water.

I can see those prophets of Baal asking, "Four barrels of water? Doesn't he know we're in the middle of a drought? Elijah! What are you going to do with all that water?"

"Pour them on the sacrifice."

"Oh, yeah? Listen, we'll get the water for you."

He had those four barrels poured over the sacrifice, and then he turned around and asked for four more barrels. Those four were poured on, and he asked for four more. So much water poured over that sacrifice that it was soaking wet, and the trench he had dug around the altar was full of water.

Then Elijah prayed a simple prayer:

> **And it came to pass at the time of the offering of the evening sacrifice, that Elijah the prophet came near, and said, Lord God of Abraham, Isaac, and of Israel, let it be known this day that thou art God in Israel, and that I am thy servant, and that I have done all these things at thy word.**
>
> **Hear me, O Lord, hear me, that this people may know that thou art the Lord God, and that thou hast turned their heart back again.**
>
> **1 Kings 18:36,37**

How interesting that Elijah said **"let it be known ... that I am thy servant."**

Why did he not say, "Let it be known that I am thy prophet. Do this, Lord, because I am your prophet, a mighty man of God"?

Even Elijah, who *was* a mighty man of God, understood that God does not move on account of one's status but on behalf of one's service. You cannot impress God with titles. What impresses Him are His servants. Do you need fire from heaven? Then cry out for it as a servant of God, and know with all your heart that He will open the heavens and bring you the miracle you need.

> **Then the fire of the Lord fell, and consumed the burnt sacrifice, and the wood, and the stones, and the dust, and licked up the water that was in the trench.**
>
> **1 Kings 18:38**

God heard his prayer of servanthood!

Afterward, Elijah told the people to grab all of the prophets of Baal and take them down to the River Jordan, where they were all killed. This incident shows a man of God in action and shows the influence of a man of God. This is the man Elisha is going to follow. We need this background on Elijah to understand Elisha and the "crowbar of God."

Elijah was still human. As amazing as all of those things are, something happened that showed the human nature in the prophet of God. As soon as Jezebel, queen of Israel and high priestess, heard that her prophets had been killed, she sent a messenger to Elijah telling him that she was going to have him killed. What did Elijah do? The man who had just called down fire from heaven ran for his life!

We all know what happened after that, right? God gave up on Elijah because he missed it, right? No! When a man of God does miracles before our eyes and then makes one mistake, why do we want to forget him?

God did not forget Elijah, did He? The Bible says God sought out Elijah, found him, and gave him some more assignments. Also, it was at this time that He assigned him a servant, someone to help him.

WHO IS THE GREATEST?

How can anyone think the church can get along without the ministry of helps, without those who wait on tables, take care of the nursery, or maintain the grounds? The Bible clearly shows us that Jesus considered Himself a servant of the Father. That means that even those in the ministry really are servants. They are simply serving at a different level of authority.

Jesus dealt with this subject when the disciples reached the place where they were arguing about rank among themselves.

Then came to him the mother of Zebedee's children with her sons, worshipping him, and desiring a certain thing of him.

And he said unto her, What wilt thou? She saith unto him, Grant that these my two sons may sit, the one on thy right hand, and the other on the left, in thy kingdom. ["Give my sons status, Lord."]

But Jesus answered and said, Ye know not what ye ask, Are ye able to drink of the cup that I shall drink of, and to be baptized with the baptism that I am baptized with? They say unto him, We are able. ["As long as we get our status." Pride, not humility, was operating.]

And he saith unto them, Ye shall drink indeed of my cup and be baptized with the baptism that I am baptized with: but to sit on my right hand, and on my left, is not mine to give, but it shall be given to them for whom it is prepared of my Father.

And when the ten heard it, they were moved with indignation against the two brethren.

But Jesus called them unto him, and said, Ye know that the princes of the Gentiles exercise dominion over them, and they that are great exercise authority upon them.

But it shall not be so among you: but whosoever will be great among you, let him be your minister;

And whosoever will be chief among you, let him be your servant:

Even as the Son of man came not to be ministered unto, but to minister, and to give his life a ransom for many.

Matthew 20:20-28

Jesus said He did not come to earth to be ministered to, but to minister and to give His life as a ransom. We need to go forth and serve.

Would you take care of a dirty house and change the dirty diapers for the children of a family of sinners so they could hear the Word of God?

Would you take food and clothing to a family that does not yet know Jesus?

Would you put someone else first and yourself second?

Lift up your head and cry out to God because our God does not move on behalf of those with status in this world but on behalf of His servants, those with humble hearts.

4

ELISHA, THE SERVANT
OF THE MAN OF GOD

Shortly after the episode with the prophets of Baal, when rain was restored to Israel, Elijah found his servant. And the man called to serve also was the man God had chosen to take Elijah's place — Elisha, son of Shaphat. (1 Kings 19:16.) When Elijah saw him, Elisha was plowing with twelve yoke of oxen. (v. 19.)

Notice that Elisha was not a poor man, or he would not have been plowing with that many oxen. When Elijah passed by him, he threw his mantle on Elisha. And Elisha left the oxen and ran after Elijah. Why did he do that?

I believe something powerful happened when the mantle fell on Elisha. I believe that mantle was the anointing, and in the anointing was a lot of love. When the anointing dropped on him, he walked away from everything he had. Something must have happened that moved Elisha very deeply.

The only thing he asked was to have time to go kiss his father and mother goodbye. But Elijah answered with a statement that, at first reading, is puzzling. When you look at the circumstances, Elijah's remark sounds very strange:

> **Go back again: for what have I done to thee?**
>
> **1 Kings 19:20**

Why did Elijah say that? What he was saying, in modern language, was: "All right, Elisha. If you are going to follow me, it will have to be between you and God. I'm not going to have anything to do with it!"

Elijah was simply obeying God and making Elisha responsible for his own decision.

We think it would be easier to follow a man of God who would say, "Hey, the Lord told me I would find you out here! He told me to throw my mantle of anointing over you because you are going to carry on as a prophet after me."

Instead, Elijah said, "Go on about your business. I have done nothing to cause you to follow me. This is between you and God."

That was the strong point offered to Elisha, "the crowbar." God offered it to him, and he took it.

> **And he (Elisha) returned back from him (Elijah), and took a yoke of oxen, and slew them, and boiled their flesh with the**

instruments of the oxen, and gave unto the people, and they did eat. Then he arose, and went after Elijah, and [take note of this phrase] ministered unto him.

1 Kings 19:21

If you study the meaning of *minister* in several different translations of the Bible, you will see that Elisha served and helped the man of God. The word *minister* means "to contribute to, to serve, to attend, and to wait upon."[1]

Elisha made his own decision. He made it while standing in the middle of a plowed field. There were no bright lights, no sweet sounds of orchestral music, no congregation present to see history being made. There was just the Lord and Elisha, for the man of God had walked on by himself.

You make decisions every day. We all do. What about this one:

"When I walked into this church, I just felt the love of God engulf me. I feel so blessed. I love this place. I tell you, this is where God wants me!"

Then two weeks later, you are nowhere to be found in that church. All of us have heard people say these kinds of things. Perhaps you have said them. Elisha's decision was not like that. He made what we call a "quality" decision, one that is settled once and for all, one that brought about a permanent change in his life.

---

[1]James Strong, *The Exhaustive Concordance of the Bible* (Nashville: Abingdon, 1890) Hebrew and Chaldee Dictionary, #8334.

DEVELOPING A CROWBAR

Elisha followed Elijah and began a lengthy term of service for the man of God. He traveled with him, looked after his clothes, cooked his meals, and did anything else necessary to free the man of God for ministry and for spiritual things.

The only reason Elisha was able to do this was because of that irrevocable decision he made in the field with the oxen. During all those years, he still was not told why he was to follow Elijah. Certainly he was tired, hot, sweaty, and dirty at times. Yet, despite any hardships, he stuck with the words he had spoken many years before.

Some Christians cannot stick with their decisions for two weeks. Then we wonder why people around us want nothing to do with our God. Instead of reflecting Jesus to the world, many of us reflect a God who looks mixed up, confused, and misguided. Who wants to serve a God like that? But we are quick to run to tell our unsaved friends when God speaks to us.

"But, Buddy," you may say, "Elisha was going to take Elijah's place."

We know that, but Elisha did not.

In all of the incidents related in the Bible about Elijah after this time, Elisha may not be mentioned, but he was there. The servant goes where the master goes. He saw all of the things God did through His man, Elijah.

In 2 Kings 1:1-2, the Word says:

> **Then Moab rebelled against Israel after the death of Ahab.**
>
> **And Ahaziah fell down through a lattice in his upper chamber that was in Samaria, and was sick: and he sent messengers, and said unto them, Go, inquire of Baalzebub the god of Ekron whether I shall recover of this disease.**

Ahaziah was the king of Israel. Yet here he was sending messengers to ask questions of a pagan god, setting an example of idolatry for the nation.

About that time, the Lord sent an angel to Elijah with some instructions. The Lord told Elijah to intercept the messengers from the king's house in Samaria, the capital of Israel, and speak certain words to them.

In today's language, this is what Elijah said:

"Are you going to the so-called god in Ekron to help you because you think there is no God in Israel? Tell King Ahaziah that because he looked for help from a strange god that he surely will die." (vv. 3,4.)

So the messengers returned to Ahaziah with Elijah's words, and he asked them what the man looked like who had given them this message.

They said, "He was a hairy man with a girdle of leather about his loins." (v. 8.)

The king knew who that was all right: **Elijah the Tishbite.**
(v. 8.)

Ahaziah sent a captain with fifty troops to capture Elijah.
They found him sitting on a hill, and the captain shouted to him to
come down because the king wanted him. But Elijah asked God
to vindicate His words.

> And Elijah answered and said to the captain of fifty, If I be a
> man of God, then let fire come down from heaven, and consume
> thee and thy fifty. And there came down fire from heaven, and
> consumed him and his fifty.

> **2 Kings 1:10**

Whoosh! All fifty-one men were gone. You need to understand
that this is not a fairy tale. This really happened. This fire is the same
kind of fire that burns up houses. This is the real thing. Elijah called
that fire down, and all fifty men plus the captain were consumed
to ashes on the spot.

A SERVANT FOLLOWS HIS MASTER

The Bible does not mention Elisha during this incident. But
how can you serve someone if you are not where he is? Elisha was
nearby because he was the servant of the man of God. Because
Elisha was human, I wonder if the thought entered his mind, like
it would enter our minds, to hope Elijah never got mad at him?

Imagine if a modern pastor suddenly stopped one Sunday morning in the pulpit and said, "If I be a man of God, let fire come down out of heaven and consume that piano." Then *whoosh!* the piano suddenly burns up, and nothing around it is touched. The doors of the church would be torn off by people trying to get out.

I do not believe Elijah had a smile on his face during this demonstration of God's power. He probably looked mean enough to chew nails.

If your pastor stood up in church with that look on his face, what would you do?

Most people would say, "This is the last Sunday I'm coming here! I'm going to some church where people preach love and show me some love."

But did you not say *God* told you to attend this church? Did you not say you *knew* this was where you were supposed to be?

"Yes, but I didn't know fire was going to be called down from heaven by the pastor!"

Human nature being the same in Bible days as today, Elisha may have had some questioning thoughts. He may even have considered finding another prophet to serve. But after some reflecting, he soon came back to the scene in the field where he was first called and to his decision to forsake all to follow Elijah.

God hasn't told me anything different, he might have thought.

So I'm going to go all the way with this service to the man of God. But I certainly am going to be more careful about what I say to him!

The king of Israel did not give up easily. After all, he probably thought if he could get rid of the prophet, he could get rid of the sentence of death passed on him. He quickly sent another 50 men with their captain. And *whoosh!* Fire came down and consumed them also. (vv. 11,12.)

Elisha was learning things he had never known before and seeing things he had never seen before. He must have been startled. Perhaps he even considered going back to farming. But Elisha remembered that he had a "crowbar," and he began to use it.

Just like Elisha, often we go through a first fire and have to face another fire coming right behind it.

One Sunday morning, your pastor may speak pretty strong words from the pulpit. Perhaps he is calling on his members to straighten up their acts, come into unity with one another, and get on with the job. You immediately get hurt and defensive but decide to give him another chance.

But the next Sunday, he does the same thing, calling forth an even stronger message. Alarmed, you suggest that your family leave the church and find another where the pastor brings messages of love from the pulpit. You need to remember who said you should be in that church to begin with. Did *you* choose it, or did God?

Elisha was living through natural circumstances just as we have to do. Elijah never placed honors on him or certified his service. He did not make life easy for his servant. The servant's place was to make life easier for the man of God. Remember, Elisha wielded his "crowbar" and was not moved by the difficulty involved with serving the prophet. He simply went on serving.

FAITHFULNESS COMES BY CHOICE

Going through the fires of life can be easier if someone pats you on the back or reassures you of your calling. But the one thing that kept Elisha going was the fact that he had made a decision to serve, and he would be true to his word.

Everyone can get excited about being part of the supernatural or about following a great man of God. We might even dream of being Elijahs or Elishas, but we need to realize that life was not all roses for Elisha. We know the result of his years of service, but Elisha did not know until Elijah was taken up into the heavens.

Ahaziah was a stubborn man, especially with his life in the balance. He sent yet a third group of fifty men with a captain to take Elijah off the hill where he was sitting. But this captain had more common sense and wisdom than the previous two.

When he got to the hill where Elijah sat, he fell on his knees and pleaded for the lives of himself and his men. Then the angel of the Lord told Elijah it was time to go with the troops, so he came down off the hill and went to visit the king in person. (2 Kings 1:13-15.)

These incidents were specialized training for Elisha. He used his crowbar and learned all of the lessons the Lord sent his way.

Ahaziah, king of Israel, soon found it had not done him any good to send after Elijah. When Elijah saw the king, he told him to his face the same thing he had said to the messengers:

> **Thou shalt not come down off that bed on which thou art gone up, but shalt surely die.**
>
> **2 Kings 1:16**

What happened to Elijah? The Bible does not tell us, but obviously, he walked out of the palace at Samaria a free man. In the very next chapter, we are told of his being taken up to heaven in a chariot of fire. We do know what happened to the king because verse 17 says,

> **So he died according to the word of the Lord which Elijah had spoken.**

Elisha had to endure all kinds of surprises. But he stayed through it all because he had made a decision. He continued to grow in every way as he abided by his own word. Elisha had plenty of opportunities to bail out. If he had not been a man of his word, a man who stuck by his decisions, he would not have become the prophet who came after Elijah in the Bible. The prophet would have been someone else.

Elisha remained with the man of God whether he spoke

judgment or blessings. Christians today get upset with those who bring correction from God or who carry "bad news." But nothing caused Elisha to waver. He used his special tool from God to stand by Elijah and to become personally all that God wanted him to be.

5

MOLDED, SHAPED, AND PREPARED FOR GOD'S TIMING

The "crowbar" Elisha used was *faithfulness*.

Faithfulness kept him at the prophet's side through every kind of adversity.

Faithfulness is the "crowbar of God."

Remember that Elisha was never told why he was to travel with Elijah. You have seen in the Scriptures that his was not an easy life. Being in service to others means your life is not your own. There were fires to pass through and things to learn, all the while doing the menial, everyday tasks that go with living.

Do you think you could watch men be consumed by fire and still serve that prophet?

Finally, at the end of Elijah's life, we see Elisha's reward.

And it came to pass, when the Lord would take up Elijah into heaven by a whirlwind, that Elijah went with Elisha from Gilgal.

And Elijah said unto Elisha, Tarry here, I pray thee; for the Lord hath sent me to Beth-el. [Then Elisha began to use his crowbar.] And Elisha said unto him, As the Lord liveth, and as thy soul liveth, I will not leave thee. So they went down to Beth-el.

2 Kings 2:1,2

Elisha had feelings like us. Did he think, *Didn't the Lord say anything about me, Elijah? I've been with you for years; I've waited upon you hand and foot. Didn't God say anything about me?*

Even if he thought that, what he said was this: "Elijah, years ago the Lord called me, and I went with you as a servant. And, as long as I live, I am going to do what He said. I will stick with you wherever you go, no matter what."

The Scriptures say they both went down to Bethel. From a quick reading of the story, it may look as if Elijah is trying to shake Elisha off his trail. Was he trying to spoil God's plan? Was he trying to go alone?

No, Elijah was molding and shaping Elisha for something special yet to come. Elisha still did not know what the outcome of his life of service for Elijah would be. People today often say they know what the Lord has in store for them. Let me tell you something: They do not know what they are saying! They could not possibly know the plans of God in detail.

44

The Lord *does* give us general directions many times, and He *does* give us specific details occasionally. But if He laid out all of His plans for our lives in detail, we would not walk by faith. He would be denying us the exercising of our faith. And *it is impossible to please God* without faith! (Heb. 11:6.)

Elisha had been prepared day by day for years for a very special service. Elijah nurtured him in faithfulness from the very beginning.

Are you willing to let God shape and mold you for something more than what you know about?

Are you willing to let God use people — men of God — to do some of the molding and shaping?

Or are you going to bail out at the first fire, or get your feelings bruised when the prophet says, "The Lord told *me* to go to Bethel, not *you*."

Are you going to be left behind?

Sometimes we excuse ourselves for disobedience in leaving the church where God put us by these kinds of excuses: "Brother Bell, I'll tell you why I don't go to that church anymore. They put a new department head over me, and I'll tell you what, that guy rubs me the wrong way!"

I would like to answer, "Well, my good friend, you must need rubbing on those wrong ways of yours, or God would not have allowed that man to be put over you!"

So, yes, you may have a glimpse of the future, but you do not have nearly the full picture. If you told me what you were going to be doing six months from now, you would just be guessing at it. The only One who knows what is going to be happening six months from now is God, and possibly the men of God, His prophets.

God is good. He knows what He is doing. Are you willing to let Him have His way with you? Are you willing to let Him prepare you for service?

> **And the sons of the prophets that were at Bethel came forth to Elisha, and said unto him, Knowest thou that the Lord will take away thy master from thy head today? And he said, Yea, I know it; hold ye your peace.**
>
> **2 Kings 2:3**

In other words, Elisha said, "I know what is going on, and I know what I'm doing. Just be quiet."

Those were the "sons (students) of the prophets." Those men were not flakes. They knew what they were talking about. And you thought you could only be tempted by evil things?

What happens when your good Christian friends come and tell you of a new church starting up? These are people you respect; they are born again and filled with the Holy Spirit. They even prophesy now and again. Are you going to follow them? Or are you going to follow the man of God you were called to follow?

TIMES OF DECISION

You have to make a decision at times like these. Are you going to stay where God put you, or are you going to try to please your friends? Elisha made a decision, but as you can see, it was not a one-time decision in practice. He had to keep reaffirming his decision throughout all of those years.

When they got to Bethel, Elijah "tried" his servant again.

He said, "Okay, you followed me this far, but you stay here now. I have to go on to Jericho. The Lord has sent me to Jericho." (2 Kings 2:4.)

Elisha once again used that crowbar of faithfulness. Once again, he reaffirmed his decision to follow the prophet. He insisted on going with Elijah to Jericho.

Many Christians think that they are to mold and shape themselves. Perhaps by attending Bible school, they think they will come out finished products for the Lord's use. But it does not take faith to mold yourself. Molding yourself is *works* — that is flesh.

Are you willing to use the crowbar of faith, deal with one day at a time, and let a man of God shape you for something that only God knows about?

Once at Jericho, Elisha again was approached by students at the school of prophets there. They asked him the same thing the others did: Did he know his master was being taken up by God that day? Elisha gave them the same answer. He seemed to be pounded with trials right to the very end, being tested by those who were good people and friends. But this was all part of the shaping and molding process.

Then Elijah said to Elisha for the third time, "You stay here now. I have to go on to the Jordan River." (2 Kings 2:6.)

Elisha had not yet been told why he was following the man of God to the very end, but he knew he would not let go. He would not leave him until God took him. Elisha was using his crowbar of faithfulness that had been developed over his years of service.

And the two men, prophet and servant, went on. Verse seven tells us that fifty sons of the prophets followed them and watched from a distance as they reached the river. They did what a lot of our well-meaning friends do. They try to stop us from doing what God is leading us to do because they think we are wrong.

If someone wrote to you today and sent you a check for several thousand dollars to go to Bible school, would you pack up the next day and leave? Would you automatically think that because this seems like a good thing, it must be God's will? Would you even consider that God already had told you something else to do for Him?

Elijah took off his mantle, folded it together, and slapped the waters of the river with it. Second Kings 2:8 says the river parted, and the two men walked across on dry land — as the Israelites had when they left Egypt just a jump ahead of Pharoah's army.

How would you react if you were standing there with Elijah? The prophet had called fire down from heaven, raised a boy from the dead, made the rain stop and begin again, and killed false prophets. He moved in the supernatural, so I am sure the parting of the waters of Jordan was no big deal to Elijah.

Then Elijah and Elisha walked across the riverbed. Elisha used his crowbar of faithfulness, telling himself that if the prophet was going, so was he. If the water came down, it would come down on both of them.

Pastors often strike the waters of a "faith venture" much to the surprise of their congregations. And they urge the whole church to come on through the "river," but many cannot make it. The waters are around them, and they shake and quake until they finally turn back.

A church can be very much like the man who set out to swim across the Mississippi River. He swam halfway, and then decided he could not make it, so he turned around and swam back! He could have made it just as easily on across, but he chose to turn back. He gave up too soon.

When the man of God shows the way, you need to grab hold of his coattails and say, "You parted the waters. I'm sticking with you. If the water comes down, it will come down on both of us."

That is the force of faithfulness. Nothing can stop it. Now look at the next verse:

And it came to pass, when they were gone over, that Elijah said unto Elisha, "Ask what I shall do for thee, before I be taken away from thee" (v. 9).

Notice that Elisha did not react the way we may think. He was not jumping up and down, shouting, and carrying on. He answered, very humbly, "I pray thee [please], let a double portion of thy spirit be upon me" (v. 9). Elisha asked this with a reverence and a fear of God. What he was about to ask for, no other man had ever asked for. I am sure that he did not even know if he would live to tell of this favor.

Elijah answered:

"Thou hast asked a hard thing: nevertheless, if thou see me when I am taken from thee, it shall be so unto thee; but if not, it shall not be so" (v. 10).

Looking at the closing of Elijah's days on earth, we see a very important concept in becoming who God wants you to be, and that is *His timing.*

Elijah was saying, "Elisha, be faithful, and in the Lord's timing, you will receive your request for a double anointing."

"You can have it in the Lord's timing" might be a bit hard for you, a modern Christian, to swallow. So even at the price of irritating you, I will ask you to consider this again:

Are you willing to let God shape you, mold you, and prepare

you so you can be ready for that time in your life?

Are you willing to step into the faith realm, and let God and the man of God (your pastor) shape and mold you into God's precious pottery?

Elisha kept a good attitude, even after all of the things he had gone through, all of the serving, all of the frustration over the previous years. None of that affected Elisha's attitude toward his master (pastor). He could have decided not to even talk to him anymore — to just let the old guy go at it alone.

There had been a cultivation process in Elisha. The man of God, Elijah, had done his job well. He had molded and prepared his servant for ministry. He did his job so well that Elisha would do even greater supernatural feats than his teacher. Elijah could leave, knowing his ministry was in good hands.

> **And it came to pass, as they still went on, and talked, that, behold, there appeared a chariot of fire, and horses of fire, and parted them both asunder; and Elijah went up by a whirlwind into heaven.**
>
> **And Elisha saw it, and he cried, My father, my father, the chariot of Israel, and the horsemen thereof. And he saw him no more: and he took hold of his own clothes, and rent them in two pieces.**
>
> **2 Kings 2: 11,12**

In the Old Testament, it is unusual for the word *father* to be used in this manner, as a term of endearment. The man of God had shown Elisha so many things, and they had grown so close over the years, that Elijah had really become like a father to Elisha. One of the many definitions of *pastor* is "father-like one." Suddenly, the man who always knew what was going on and what was to be done, had left Elisha without companionship and the security that comes with leaning on another in authority.

The Scriptures tell us, however, that Elisha then took up the mantle of Elijah, walked back to the riverbank, and smote the waters just as his "father-like one" had done. He had grown in faithfulness. His "crowbar" had become a tool for success, and God's timing now rested on him.

FAITHFULNESS KEEPS YOU HUMBLE

If you want faithfulness to take over in your life, then allow God to use the people set over you to form you into something useful. Start by being faithful where you are, in the little things. Make a decision, and be a man or woman of your word.

Elisha's faithfulness took over in his life. He had grown to the place where nothing else mattered. His faithfulness was in control. Now he had the mantle of the "father-like one," and as he hit the water, he said, **"Where is the Lord God of Elijah?"** (2 Kings 2:14).

The "Lord God of Elijah" answered him, the waters parted, and Elisha went back over the Jordan to where the sons of the prophets waited.

As Elisha entered his own ministry, he remembered all that he had learned in his service to Elijah and walked on. When God is leading you to do something, He usually tells you just enough to get you going in the right direction. You are always required to trust Him and have faith in Him. God will tell you when to start using the crowbar He has given you.

Pry yourself out of that easy chair to go to church on Sunday and on weeknights. Let God shape and mold you into what He wants. You have specialties for Him that only you can give Him. You will find God's will for your life with the help of your crowbar and your pastor. The crowbar belongs to you, however. Your pastor cannot use it for you. Only you can keep yourself in faith.

Years from now, the Lord may lead you in another direction. But for now, serve in your church. When you get into tomorrow, you are not in faith. Faith is now. Faith is for today. Christianity is exciting! You do not know what may happen from one day to the next.

If you are bored with your Christian walk, perhaps you are trying to mold and shape yourself. Faith is the thing that pleases God. And when you charge up with faith, things begin to move and happen. The boredom will leave as you serve.

Once, I wanted to leave a church where God had put me. There were many occasions when I wanted to leave because I did not understand the things the pastor did to me. I would cry on my wife's shoulder about why "they" did not think I was faithful and why "they" were always testing my faithfulness.

Then I would remember the day in church when God seemed to open up and pour His supernatural love down inside of me. A mantle was dropped on me, and I could not sit in church anymore. I had to be involved. I did whatever I was asked to do. I was laughed at and mocked. I wanted to quit a thousand times, but I am a man of my word. I would not quit.

People would ask me, "Buddy, when are you going to leave the church and start your own ministry? You have *such* an anointing."

That was soothing to my ears at first, especially when the pastor had pointed his finger at me for doing something wrong. Then it sounded really good! But I was reminded of Elisha saying, **"As the Lord liveth, and as thy soul liveth"** (2 Kings 2:2), and I would reaffirm my resolve to serve my pastor. That was where God wanted me, in order to mold and shape me into what He wanted me to be.

God is the Potter, and we are the clay. Surrendering completely to His molding and shaping is scary sometimes and not always enjoyable. Somehow, we always feel we can do the job much better — although we *know* that we cannot.

But we are not to run our lives on the way we feel but on what the Word of God says.

You can make the same decision I did: not to run anymore. You will find a peace, a joy, and more faithfulness than you have ever dreamed of from making that decision. You just need to grab your "crowbar." It is there, ready-made just for you. You will be staying under the anointing of the ministry of helps, and you have the ability to do supernatural things.

Second Kings 3:11-12 says:

> But Jehoshaphat said, Is there not here a prophet of the Lord, that we may enquire of the Lord by him? And one of the king of Israel's servants answered and said, Here is Elisha the son of Shaphat, which poured water on the hands of Elijah (who was the servant of that great man of God, Elijah).
>
> And Jehoshaphat said, The Word of the Lord is with him.

Elisha, the one who was faithful!

6

BEING ABOUT
OUR FATHER'S BUSINESS:
JESUS AND THE MINISTRY
OF HELPS, PART 1

It's amazing how many people actually think that Jesus did everything Himself. I know many church people think that way because in my travels, I see firsthand how congregations expect their pastors to do it all.

They can't help that kind of thinking. They've been taught what I call "incomplete pictures" from the Bible, showing that Jesus did everything Himself. But that is not a fact. Even Jesus had the ministry of helps. In these next two chapters, we're going to see how valuable the ministry of helps was to Jesus and why it is still needed today.

In my travels, I met a pastor in a restaurant who knew nothing about the helps ministry. When I tried to explain it to him, he got a fearful look in his eyes and told me that if I taught that in his church, he would lose his paycheck. Pastors need to pastor in faith if they're going to be effective, but too often they pastor in fear. Their messages are motivated by fear, and their congregations have put that fear upon them. What's sad is that in many cases we've used the Word of God to do it.

> And he gave some, apostles; some, prophets; and some, evangelists; and some, pastors and teachers; for the perfecting of the saints, for the work of the ministry, for the edifying of the body of Christ: till we all come in the unity of the faith, and of the knowledge of the Son of God, unto a perfect man, unto the measure of the stature of the fulness of Christ.
>
> Ephesians 4:11-13

Some believers read those verses and think they are referring only to pastors; so they stop reading at "for the work of the ministry, for the edifying of the body of Christ." In their minds, this passage gives three things pastors are supposed to be doing:

1. The perfecting of the saints;

2. The work of the ministry;

3. The edifying of the body of Christ.

Actually, verse 12 states three purposes for the five ministry gifts that are mentioned in verse 11. Yet so often these verses are brought up to pastors before they are hired. The scenario often goes something like this:

The hiring committee, made up of the elders and the deacon board, usually has a meeting with the prospective pastor. During the meeting they say, "Pastor, we want to get a few things straight before you take over the church here, and we would like to use the Bible to show you what we expect out of you, and what God expects out of you."

Then they proceed to read Ephesians 4:11-12 and say, "We see in this passage that God has given you to us. Do you understand that? Good. Now, let's see what you're supposed to be doing as our pastor."

"First of all, verse 12 says that you are here for the perfecting of the saints. In other words, we expect you to get up on the platform on Sunday mornings and evenings, on Wednesday nights, and whenever else we tell you to and minister the Word of God. Do you understand that? Good. Let's go to number two."

"The second point is that you are here for the work of the ministry. That means doing church-related work in addition to preaching the Word on Sundays and Wednesdays. Our last pastor seemed to have a problem in that area, but we know you won't have that problem, will you?"

When the prospective pastor shakes his head, they continue, "The Bible clearly states here that if you'll do these two things, the body of Christ will be edified. In other words, we will be happy."

Pastors have told me that this is exactly what happened to them. Anyone who subjects a pastor to that kind of hiring process is putting fear upon them. That pastor knows one thing for sure— they had better do the work of the ministry or they may lose their position. Looking at those verses in that way makes the ministry of the pastor an overly burdensome calling.

How sad that some pastors are put under that kind of fear and pressure, especially with the Word of God. One of the reasons pastors are hired initially is because they are anointed, powerful preachers. That's what the people like about them. But when they are expected to take care of all the work of the ministry, that means they will have to stop reading the Word and spending time in prayer (which is how they got the preaching anointing in the first place). Inevitably, they will lose the power and anointing to preach effectively.

So the pastor is caught in a vicious cycle of trying to do all the work of the ministry and preaching in all the services and meetings. If that continues, eventually they will start to slack up on doing the work of the ministry so they can spend time again in the Word and prayer and get back the anointing to preach. Within a few months, the people will come to them and say, "Pastor, you seem to be falling behind on the work of the ministry. Is there a problem?" and the pastor can't win for losing.

Can you see why so many wonderful, powerful men and women of God have thrown in the towel? They feel pulled in so many directions that they finally say, "Forget it. Maybe I'm not called to be a pastor. I can't get it together. I get ahead over here and I get behind over there. I try to catch up over there and I get behind over here," and they quit.

Let me help you understand exactly what the Word of God is saying in Ephesians 4.

LIFTING UP JESUS

We just saw in verse 11 that, "He gave some apostles, some prophets, some evangelists, some pastors and teachers." Do you know why God gave us pastors? It's not to boss them around or to keep them poor in order to see if living a life of faith really works. That is actually how some Christians interpret this passage. Of course, neither of those is true.

The answer can be found in verse 12. Let's read it from *The Amplified Bible:* "His [God's] intention was the perfecting and the full equipping of the saints (His consecrated people), [that they should do] the work of ministering toward building up Christ's body (the church)."

Why are we, the saints of God, being perfected and equipped by our pastors (who God has set in the church) to do the work of the ministry? "For the edifying of the body of Christ" (KJV). That word *edify* means to build up or to promote "another's growth in Christian wisdom...happiness, holiness."[1]

Promoting others begins by first lifting up Jesus. In John 12:32, Jesus told us, "If I be lifted up...*I will draw all men unto me.*" *Lifted up* means "to exalt, to raise to dignity, honor."[2] How are we lifting up Jesus in church? Some church members think that it's by having the pastor do more work around the church—painting Sunday school rooms or mowing the grass. But I truly believe the answer has been here all the time.

The ministry gifts cannot lift up Jesus all by themselves. Pastors cannot do it all alone. The church staff cannot do it by themselves. They need the members to do the work of the ministry, which is what they are equipping us to do!

If we will allow the ministry gifts to do their part—to perfect and to equip us with the Word—then we can begin to do our part (the work of the ministry). That will free up the pastor to accomplish their part, and others will be drawn to Christ.

You might say, "That's just you. You're hung up on this work thing. You think and breathe and live the ministry of helps. You just work in church all the time." The truth is, Jesus functioned this way.

[1] Thayer and Smith, *The KJV New Testament Greek Lexicon*, "Greek Lexicon entry for Oikodome," S.V. "edifying," Ephesians 4:12, available from <http://www.biblestudytools.net/Lexicons/Greek/grk.cgi?number=3619&version=kjv>.
[2] Ibid., "Greek Lexicon entry for Hupsoo," s.v. "lifted up," John 12:32, available from <http://www.biblestudytools.net/Lexicons/Greek/grk.cgi?numbers=5312&version=kjv>.

THE GREAT SHEPHERD

In His ministry, Jesus was our example of the ministry gifts in Ephesians 4. Do you know which one He was noted for, the one that stood out from the others? Some people say *teacher*. Others say *prophet*. But Jesus was not known as the great apostle or the great prophet or the great teacher or the great evangelist, even though He was all of those. He was known as the Great Shepherd.

The word *shepherd* is often used symbolically in the Bible to refer to *pastor*. Unfortunately, the ministry gift of pastor is thought of by some as the low gift on the totem pole. We talk about apostles, and we have that far off look in our eyes. We talk about prophets and evangelists, and we get a look of excitement on our faces. We talk about teachers, and we have that studious look. Why is it that when we talk about pastors, we have the "they're a dime a dozen" look? Nothing could be further from the truth!

Pastors are an essential part of the five ministry gifts, and Jesus was the prime example. On His way to the cross, He preached and taught and loved people. He had compassion for them and healed them, yet He didn't function without the ministry of helps. The disciples helped Jesus fulfill His purpose and vision on earth.

Most pastors have a vision, a purpose, and goals; Jesus was no different. When I've posed the question in churches, "What was Jesus' goal on earth?" I've heard a variety of answers:

• He was here to fulfill the Father's will.

• He was here to reveal God to us.

• He was here to serve us.

• He was here to redeem us to the Father.

How do we know He did all that? His goal was to get to the cross. If He didn't make it to the cross, none of the rest would have happened. That was His purpose here on earth and, thank God, He made it to the cross. But do you know how He made it?

Many people don't realize that certain things had to be completed in an allotted time and biblical prophecies had to be fulfilled before God would allow Jesus to be nailed to the cross. We're going to delve into some of these conditions now because they illustrate God's biblical structure for the church.

One Bible passage gives the account of something significant that happened on the way to the cross—the feeding of the multitude. I'm sure that the way you've heard this story taught was that Jesus fed the multitude, and all He had were five loaves of bread and two fishes. The way the picture has been painted to us is that Jesus did it all.

Five thousand men plus women and children were waiting to be fed, and Jesus took the five loaves and two fishes, looked up to heaven and blessed them, broke the fish and the loaves, and fed over five thousand people. But this account is not completely true. Jesus didn't do it all by Himself. He had the ministry of helps around Him.

I'm going to complete the picture of what happened that day. Keep in mind Ephesians 4:11-13 as we take a closer look at this story.

"YOU FEED THEM"

After Jesus received the news of John the Baptist's beheading, He left by boat to be alone. But a multitude of people heard of His departure and followed Him on land. When He went ashore and saw the great amount of people waiting for Him, He had compassion for them and held a healing service. As evening approached, it was obvious that the people would need to eat soon.

The twelve disciples came to Jesus and said, "This is a desert place, and the time is now past; send the multitude away, that they may go into the villages, and buy themselves victuals [food]" (Matt. 14:15).

The twelve had this great idea about how the people should get food to eat, and they told Jesus what He ought to do. But Jesus answered the twelve, "They need not depart. Give ye them to eat." (Matt. 14:16.) In other words, "You feed them." Was Jesus being irresponsible? No, He knew that we have to be moving forward in service, doing our part, to be overtaken with blessings!

How did the disciples respond? The twelve said to the One (Jesus), "We have here but five loaves, and two fishes." (Matt. 14:17.)

Have you ever heard that type of statement made in your church? "Pastor, you want to build what kind of addition to this building? Have you looked at our checking account lately?"

What did the One say to the twelve? "All right, men. I'll tell you what. I'll go and feed the first two thousand people just to show you that this is really going to work. Just hang in there with Me, and I'll even feed twenty-five hundred people to prove to you that it works."

Of course, Jesus didn't say or do that, but how often is that version played out in modern-day churches? The deacons stand back and say, "Okay, Pastor. We've told you what to do, and you won't follow our advice. So we all agree that you should do it, and maybe we'll jump in and help out. We'll see if it works first." So pastors end up doing most or all of the work, which prevents them from being able to focus on what God called them to do, and the multitude never gets fed.

In this biblical account, Jesus didn't handle things all by Himself. He told the disciples to sit the multitude down near Him in groups of a hundred and groups of fifty. (Mark 6:39,40.) This struck me as a very interesting move on Jesus' part.

Once while teaching this message in a church, I said, "If I were to ask you to sit these people down in groups of tens or twenties, how would you do it?" One person responded, "Count them off one at a time." That was a good answer because after you've done that, you would be able to tell me exactly how many people were sitting down; there would be no guessing about it.

When I read this for the first time, I thought, *Jesus, that's not too smart. The disciples already know that all they have are five loaves and two fishes to feed this multitude. If You have them seat all those people in groups of a hundred and groups of fifty, they're going to know exactly how many people are out there, and they're going to get upset at the large number that need to be fed. You would be better off keeping them guessing as to the actual amount.*

But that would not be perfecting the saints, would it? Remember, our pastors are here to perfect us, just as Jesus was perfecting the disciples.

KEEPING RIGHT ATTITUDES

After the thousands of people had been seated on the grass, Matthew 14:19 says that Jesus "took the five loaves, and the two fishes, and looking up to heaven, He blessed, and broke, *and gave the loaves to His disciples*, and the disciples to the multitude."

Who passed out the food? It's clear from this verse that Jesus didn't. The disciples passed out the food. The Bible goes on to say that the people "did all eat, and were filled: and they (the disciples) took up of the fragments that remained twelve baskets full."

Let's back up for a moment. We saw that the disciples told Jesus what to do, and He said, "No, this is what you're going to do." Now remember that according to Ephesians 4:11-12, the ministry gifts are here to perfect and equip the saints so the saints can do the work of the ministry. When those two things are being done properly, the body of Christ will be edified. Can you see it unfolding in this story? Jesus is perfecting the saints—in this case, the disciples.

I also want you to notice that Jesus is not doing much running around. He is saying to the disciples, "*You* go get the food and bring it to Me. *You* pass it out." Then the disciples did as Jesus said and brought the food to Him. What did He do? He took the food, looked up to heaven, blessed it, broke it, and handed it back to the same men who had told Him what to do—the ones who knew exactly how many people were sitting out on that hillside. I believe that at that moment there was an opportunity for some unsaintly attitudes to surface!

Imagine the disciples standing there, looking at the five loaves of bread and two fishes, and knowing how many people were out there waiting to be fed. They stare at Jesus, they glance at the food, then they look at the multitude. I believe at this point some interesting thoughts are going through their heads. *Maybe we ought to eat first. These people just show up every now and then. We're with the Lord all the time. If anybody ought to go through the line first, it ought to be the staff.*

Isn't that what often happens in churches? The staff goes

through the line first, and they take the best of everything. Then, when the multitude comes in behind them, the multitude often doesn't get enough to eat.

How long would it take to pass out food to approximately 15,000 people? Could the disciples do it in five minutes? Ten minutes? Half an hour? An hour? It probably took several hours to pass out that food—and that was several hours to develop a bad attitude.

I can just imagine the disciples passing out bread and fish, thinking, *We told Jesus what to do. Why didn't He listen? What if we run out of food? So far, every time we reach in the basket, there's something in it. But we're probably going to run out soon. We should've eaten before we started passing out the food. Look how many people we've got left to feed! At this rate, there isn't going to be anything left for us to eat.*

Surely some of the disciples had those kinds of thoughts. After all, they were facing a big problem, and they were human just like you and me. But notice that they didn't say anything. Those thoughts were coming at them, but they threw them back down every time.

You're going to have problems too. That's just a fact of life. God's going to be there with you because He never leaves you or forsakes you (Heb. 13:5), but you must decide what you're going to do with your problems. Negative thoughts will pop up in your mind during troubling times, but what you do with those thoughts determines the outcome.

The apostle Paul tells us that we're supposed to cast down all evil imaginations. (2 Cor. 10:5.) If we cast them down and refuse to dwell on them, then we won't speak them. It's when we start speaking them out loud that they grab hold of us and become a part of us. Then we've really got a problem! That's why the disciples didn't talk. They just passed out the food.

Picture the scene for a moment. The disciples begin walking toward the front of the crowd when they finish handing out the food, and Jesus is standing by twelve baskets with a smile on His face.

At this point the disciples have another opportunity for a bad attitude. Jesus tells them to gather up the remaining fragments of leftovers and put them in those twelve baskets, so they're beginning to wonder, *Now He wants us to pick up all the food that's left over? When are we going to eat?*

Have you ever wondered why there were twelve baskets left that day? Why weren't there sixteen? Why weren't there twenty-one or eight or two? Why twelve? I'm convinced the reason is that there were twelve disciples, and each basket was for each disciple.

At the end of a miracle you may forget that you had a part in that miraculous event, or you may think that God didn't really notice that you had a part in it. But God knows right where you are and exactly what you're doing at all times, and He's got many blessings waiting for you—especially when you keep a right attitude. All you need to do is get ready for heaven to open up and pour you out your basketful!

GET INVOLVED

Imagine that you are one of the disciples that day. Let's say that you've been passing out food for several hours and every time you've reached into the basket, you've pulled out some bread and fish. Now you've come to number 15,000. Maybe this last person is your spouse. You reach into your basket and pull out a fish and a loaf of bread—number 15,000.

How would that have affected you? How would you have reacted? What would you have felt on the inside? I know it would have greatly encouraged my faith in God because when I get involved, I don't think about myself anymore; I only think about God and how wonderful He is!

Here's another scenario to consider. Suppose you were there that day, but you were just standing off to the side, observing Jesus watch your pastor give out the food. Your pastor has been passing out food all day and finally comes to number 15,000. This time they motion to you to reach into the basket and pull out bread and fish. You do it and hand it to number 15,000. What would that have done to you? It wouldn't be the same as watching your pastor do it, would it?

Yes, the pastor could do everything, and the church staff could do everything; but when *you* are involved, when *you* reach into that basket and pull out the fish and the bread and hand it to number 15,000, it does more to you than if you just stand back and watch the pastor and the staff do it all.

How important is it to get involved in church and be a part of reaching the multitude? It may make you feel good to sit back and watch people getting saved and lives changed, but if you're involved in the church and you have a part in changing those lives, it does something more to you—it changes your life as well.

Do you see Ephesians 4:11-12 in this story? Are you noticing how much work of the ministry Jesus is doing? He is doing His part.

He spoke it.

He delegated it.

He blessed it.

What did the disciples do? At first, they thought they knew best and told the Great Shepherd how they thought it should be done. But they ended up doing it His way.

They got the food.

They seated the people, which probably took at least an hour.

They passed out the food, which probably took several hours.

They picked up the fragments that remained, and that probably took several more hours.

The point is, when the disciples did their part, Jesus was able to do His part. A miracle took place, and the disciples received a great blessing.

Sometimes churches look at how many members they have and compare that number to the overall population of their city. Say a church has about fifteen hundred people. The leaders look at their city of two-million-plus people and think, *We're such a small church. How could we ever reach the multitudes?* But it's simple. When believers are willing to do the work of the ministry and allow pastors to do their part, there's no telling what can happen—even feeding a multitude with only five loaves and two fishes.

STUDY NOTES

Jesus and the Ministry of Helps, Part 1

1. Read Ephesians 4:11-12. When believers misunderstand these verses, what are the three things they believe their pastor is to accomplish in their church? Explain each task in detail.
2. What is the reason pastors are usually hired? Why do most pastors quit the ministry?

Lifting Up Jesus

3. What does Ephesians 4:11-12 really require of pastors? Of congregation members?
4. What are believers doing when they lift up Jesus? What does *edify* mean to you in everyday, practical terms?

The Great Shepherd

5. As the Great Shepherd or Pastor, did Jesus do everything Himself?

6. What was His primary goal and purpose during His lifetime on earth?

"You Feed Them"

7. Read Matthew 14:14-21 and Mark 6:34-44. Who actually fed the five thousand and their families?

8. What was the first practical thing Jesus asked the disciples to do before distributing the food? Why do you think Jesus asked the disciples to do this?

Keeping Right Attitudes

9. Explain how Ephesians 4:11-12 unfolded by the account of feeding the multitude with the loaves and fishes.

10. At what points in the account could the disciples have been tempted to have bad attitudes? Can you relate to them in these situations?

11. How do you avoid having a wrong attitude? Name examples in your own life where having the wrong attitude hindered God's blessing or keeping a right attitude brought God's blessings into your life.

Get Involved

12. What happens to your thinking when you get involved in the ministry of helps? How does getting involved affect your life?

13. From the account of the loaves and fishes, how important is it to follow the specific instructions of your leaders in the church?

7

JESUS AND THE
MINISTRY OF HELPS, PART 2

L et's look at something else that happened to Jesus on the way to the cross.

> And when he [Jesus] was entered into a ship, His disciples
> followed him, And behold, there arose a great tempest of the sea,
> insomuch that the ship was covered with the waves: but he [Jesus]
> was asleep. And his disciples came to him and awoke him, saying,
> Lord, save us: we perish. And he saith unto them, Why are ye
> fearful, O ye of little faith? Then he arose, and rebuked the winds
> and the sea; and there was a great calm. But the men marveled,
> saying, What manner of man is this, that even the winds and the
> sea obey Him!

Matthew 8:23-27

It is obvious here that Jesus is a leader, but I can remember having a different impression of Him when I was little. I would be watching television and flipping through the stations, and every now and then I would come across a movie that was about Jesus and the disciples. Or I would be reading books and seeing pictures of Jesus and the disciples, and I had this image of Jesus as being tall and pale with long hair. I pictured the disciples as a tight-knit group of guys who followed about ten or twelve feet behind Him.

Back then, I imagined Jesus in Matthew 8 came up to the dock, stepped into the boat, and the disciples were right behind Him. He told them, "All right, guys. Come on. We're going to go across the lake to the other side. I have some work to do over there, and you can ride along and watch. Get in. Watch your step. Let's try to even out the seating here—half of you on this side, the other half on that side."

"It's a beautiful day to be out on the sea. Are we ready? Okay now, *I'm going to row the boat,*" and Jesus grabbed the oars and started rowing. Soon He said, "What did you say? The wind's picking up? There's a storm brewing? Just hang on. I'll row faster."

So many pastors relate to my childhood version of this story, particularly when storms come up in their church and they hear, "This is your boat. Let's see you get it to the other side." But that isn't what we read in the Bible. What really happened that day?

Jesus stepped into the boat all right, but He didn't sit down and grab the oars. He went to the rear (Mark 4:38), made a bed, and lay down to rest because He knew He was going to have to minister when He got to the other side.

I believe some negative thoughts went through a few of the disciples' heads when He did this. I can just see them looking at one another, thinking, *What's He doing? I mean, these oars will fit His hands just like they fit ours. It's His idea to go across the lake anyway.*

That would have been no different than hearing someone in your church say, "Does anybody know the pastor's whereabouts? It's his idea to come down here and do all this work and paint all these rooms. He's probably home taking a nap, listening to a Buddy Bell message."

But notice the Bible doesn't mention that the disciples said anything about Jesus. They may have had a few bad thoughts, but they didn't speak them out. Instead, *they* grabbed those oars and started rowing the boat.

Soon the wind came up, the storm began to rage, and the disciples began to fear. So they went to the stern of the ship and woke up a Man who was getting His rest. They woke up a rested Man, and that rested Man came up on deck, pointed His finger at the storm, rebuked it—and the storm ceased.

When we go to sleep at night, we go to sleep to get some rest. Maybe we have to go to work the next day, we have a special meeting to attend where we will be ministering, or we have something else on our list of things to do that requires us to be totally rested. Jesus knew He had to minister when He got to the other side of the lake. So He went to the back of the boat and got some rest.

The point is that the disciples woke up a rested Man; and that rested Man was able to come up to the bow, speak three words to the storm and turbulent waves, and put an end to a bad situation.

You may not be aware of what pastors who have to "row the boat" themselves go through. Without a competent ministry of helps working with them, they become overworked and less effective. They never get enough rest to make up for all the work they are doing. Let's take a moment to see what could easily be a typical week for this kind of pastor.

WHO'S ROWING THE BOAT IN MOST CHURCHES TODAY?

Monday morning, the phone rings. It's Sister Jones wanting to know, "Pastor Joe, were you preaching at me Sunday morning? It seemed as though every time you made a point, you were looking right at me." Now Pastor Joe's already got a long list of things to do, but he takes the time to explain that he wasn't preaching just to her.

As soon as he hangs up the phone, it rings again. This time it's Brother Jenkins, who has the same question. So he has to go through the whole explanation again. Now he's really behind schedule, and he has to run across town to a discount store to get toilet paper and light bulbs for the church. He tries to make up for the lost time on the phone, but he isn't able to do it. As a result, on Tuesday, Wednesday, Thursday, and Friday mornings, he's up early, but he's behind schedule and still has a long "To Do" list.

He's got to pick up some supplies, get the mail from the post office box, visit Brother Smith in the hospital, and mow the lawn (or shovel the snow). He runs here; he runs there. He takes care of this; he takes care of that. And somehow he has to prepare and preach a message at the Wednesday night church service.

Saturday morning, he wakes up and prays that no one will call him that day. Then he will have time to study for the Sunday message. Suddenly the phone rings. He answers and it's Brother Thompson, who proceeds to tell him that he's at the church. Pastor Joe says, "What are you doing down there? Oh, you're having a meeting? You're going to paint the Sunday school rooms? Yes, I've got paint brushes and a ladder. You want me to come down there? But today is Saturday, and I've got to get something together to preach tomorrow. What? Okay, I'll get it out of a book."

Pastor Joe hangs up the phone, goes down to a meeting he didn't call, and he starts painting the Sunday school rooms. When evening comes, everybody leaves because tomorrow's Sunday, and they go to church in the morning. But Pastor Joe stays to complete the paint job and clean up. He doesn't get home until late that night.

When he finally comes home, Pastor Joe's wife is still up. She's kept his dinner warm. He walks in very hungry because he hasn't had a decent meal all week. He's extremely tired because he's been running around too much every day. Before he sits down to eat, he looks over at the couch and realizes how worn out he is from all that he's been doing. Does he eat or does he rest? He walks over, drops on the couch, and immediately falls into a deep sleep.

Pastor Joe is awakened abruptly when the phone rings. Another church member is calling, this time with a question about the book of Revelation. He stays up late that night discussing everything this church member has concerns about. When he finally hangs up the phone, it's early Sunday morning, so he doesn't go to sleep. He takes a shower and gets dressed because he's got to get down to the church early. Why? He has the only key to the building, and some of the church members don't like sitting in their cars waiting for the church to open.

Soon it's time for the service to start. Pastor Joe comes up to the platform (the boat deck). He's tired and worn out and hasn't been in the Word all week. He steps behind the podium, looks out across the congregation (the sea). He sees the wind blowing and the storm raging (all the strife and jealousy and other problems of the people) sitting in the seats.

What does Pastor Joe do? He hasn't had time to be in the Word or to be in prayer. He hasn't had time to get any rest. So he looks at the storm and the wind and thinks, *Oh my God. What am I going to do? God, forgive me. I know I should've been in the Word. I know*

I should've been in prayer. But I had to go do this and take care of that. They wanted me to do all those things. God, forgive me.

Pastor Joe doesn't know that the Bible speaks of a different way of doing things. The pastors God envisions have the ministry of helps rowing the boat across the sea for them. They don't have to go running everywhere during the week or take care of everything themselves or come in to meetings they don't know anything about. They have help.

They don't have to paint all the buildings and add on a third story with their own hands. The ministry of helps is doing these things. They don't have to come in early on Sundays and Wednesdays and clean up the nursery and the church. The ministry of helps is taking care of it—rowing the boat across the sea—and *they've* got their own keys to the building.

When these pastors come to church on Sundays and Wednesdays, they can't wait until it's time for the service so they can get up to the podium and preach. They have been in the Word. They have been in prayer. They have had a good night's sleep and are rested. They are thinking, *Hurry up with those announcements. Release me and let me get to preaching!*

When they are introduced, they leap up behind the podiums (on deck). They look out across their congregations (the sea) and see the wind blowing and the storm raging (all the strife and jealousy and problems). But they plant their feet upon the solid rock of Jesus

Christ, point their fingers at the enemy, and rebuke the wind and the storm with the Word of God. Then the peace that passes all understanding (Phil. 4:7) permeates their churches because they have had time to be in the Word and in prayer during the week. They have had time to rest and sleep as well.

Can you see why the ministry of helps is so important? Did you see how much ministry work Jesus did? In this case, it was necessary for Him to take a nap while the disciples rowed the boat across the sea. Here's another time when Jesus did His part, the disciples did their part, and a miracle happened as a result. When they got to the other side, Jesus delivered two demon-possessed people, and they were set free. (Matt. 8:28-33.) Some church folk can't even "row" the Gospel across the road to their neighbors to set them free!

More miracles took place while Jesus was on His way to the cross because the Great Shepherd and His helps team were cooperating with each other. Imagine what could happen if the modern church operated that way.

LEADING THE DONKEY

Years ago, I was an usher in the church I was attending, and we who were in the ministry of helps decided to do something special for our pastor. On Sunday mornings, we would drive him to church. Unfortunately, there were some people who had a problem with that. They thought that he had asked us to do it. But it was strictly voluntary. We wanted to do it for him. Let me tell you why.

There is something that can easily happen to anyone when driving to church on Sunday mornings. When we leave the house, many times we're praising the Lord. But by the time we get to church, we aren't praising the Lord anymore. We are mad at the devil! Maybe someone cuts us off on the road or takes the parking spot we were headed for in the church parking lot. We cry out, "You're not going to believe what this woman did to me at the corner!" or "Wait till you hear what happened to me in the parking lot!"

The Bible says that the devil comes to steal, to kill, and to destroy, and that we're not to give place to him. (John 10:10 and Eph. 4:27.) So, we decided that we were not going to give the devil any opportunity to steal the message in our pastor's heart by getting his mind on something else. James 1:8 says that a double-minded person is unstable in all his ways. We wanted the best out of our pastor. We wanted him to be perfectly in tune with the Holy Spirit when he ministered to us on Sundays.

We told our pastor, "You sit in the back seat and read your Bible and pray. We'll take care of the devil, and we'll get you to church on time. You just stay hooked up to heaven and on what God has in your heart because we want 110 percent from you on Sunday mornings."

Some people had a problem with that, but there's actually Scripture on it. There's a story in the Bible that says Jesus didn't drive His donkey in to Jerusalem. The disciples led His donkey in.

> **And when they drew nigh unto Jerusalem, and were come to Bethphage, unto the Mount of Olives, then sent Jesus two disciples.**
>
> **Matthew 21:1**

I don't know if you have been noticing this, but Jesus is really big into delegating.

> **Saying unto them, Go into the village over against you, and straightway ye shall find an ass tied, and a colt with her: loose them, and bring them unto me. And if any man say ought unto you, ye shall say, The Lord hath need of them; and straightway he will send them.**
>
> **Matthew 21:2,3**

The two disciples didn't stand there and say, "Jesus, why don't You go get Your own donkey? You go over there and say, 'The Lord has need of them.'" No. They had the right attitude. Perhaps they knew that this was more than just their Pastor being bossy.

> **All this was done, that it might be fulfilled which was spoken by the prophet.**
>
> **Matthew 21:4**

Now wait a minute. You mean this wasn't Jesus' idea to do this? No, this wasn't Jesus' idea. He was fulfilling Bible prophecy. (Zech. 9:9.) He was doing the will of God. Some people think that pastors sit in their offices all day just thinking up things for people to do: "Is that all they do, just come up with these ideas? When do we get a break?" But pastors are continuously seeking the will of God for their church. Their primary concern is that their people be happy and successful in the perfect will of the Lord.

Pastors stand on the platform on Sunday mornings and tell their congregations what they need to say and do when they get in certain situations. They assure them from God's Word that He will deliver them. But some people have a bad attitude about it and say to themselves, *They think I'm going to do what they say, but they don't work where I work. They don't live where I live.* Thank God the two disciples didn't get into that kind of thinking when their Pastor gave them direction.

> **The disciples went and did just as Jesus had instructed them, and brought the donkey and the colt, and laid their coats on them; and He sat on the coats.**
>
> **Matthew 21:6,7 NASB**

I want to point out something else that I believe is going to help you. I don't know if you noticed this, but the two disciples brought Jesus a brand-new donkey, one that had never been ridden. They didn't get Him an old, worn-out, beat-up-looking donkey. What am I saying? It's okay for pastors to drive a nice car.

Donkeys were the mode of travel in that day just as cars are for us today. Why do we expect our pastors to drive around in an old, beat-up car that has bald tires and smells horrible? Let me tell you, a new donkey smells differently than a used donkey, and a new car smells differently than a used one. But some people have a problem when a pastor gets a new car.

What did Jesus do when they brought a donkey that no one had ridden before to Him? He got on the donkey, but He didn't drive the donkey into town. The disciples led the donkey into town, helping Jesus to fulfill His calling and to make it to the cross.

COME TO THEIR NEED

We can also see the part that Jesus' ministry of helps played in the story of the blind man who sat alongside the road. This is how it is usually taught. One day blind Bartimaeus heard that Jesus of Nazareth was passing by, and as Jesus was walking down the street, he cried out, "Thou son of David, have mercy on me" (Mark 10:48). When Jesus heard his cry, He stopped in His tracks, walked over to Bartimaeus, laid His hands on him, and healed his eyes.

Of course, that's not exactly how it happened, but it's the incomplete picture that some preachers paint for people. What's been left out here is often not taught or emphasized when this story is told. I believe that it's another example of the most important key to church growth.

When Jesus walked along the road, Bartimaeus heard that He was coming and shouted, "Thou son of David, have mercy on me!" Jesus heard his cry and stopped in His tracks. But here's the difference, and it's the key to the way the church growth ought to function. Jesus said, "Bring him to Me," and the disciples came to the blind man's side.

Surely the disciples had some thoughts about this procedure and could have developed a bad attitude by speaking them out. When Jesus gave that command, they could have said to Him, "Why can't You walk over there? The man is blind and he's calling for You, Pastor. You should go visit him."

Or they could have told the blind man what many in churches today believe: "I don't know why He has to have a prayer line at the end of every service. I'd like to get out of here early, but that won't happen. Just stand there, Bartimaeus. He'll be over here in a moment." Then we wonder why miracles happen in so few of our churches!

The disciples didn't talk that way to Jesus, and they didn't say those words to Bartimaeus. They said, "Be of good cheer, the Master calls for thee" (v. 49). I believe that they knew before Bartimaeus got what he needed that he was going to get it.

They spoke positive, encouraging words to someone in need, words that meant, "You've got questions, and you're going to get an answer. You've got a need, and it's going to be met."

Then they brought him to Jesus, who said to Bartimaeus, "Go thy way; thy faith hath made thee whole," and immediately that blind man received his sight.

How many times have people come to their pastor and said, "Pastor, I have a relative (a friend, a neighbor, etc.) who really needs Jesus, and if you would just stop by and visit with them or have coffee with them sometime, I know they would come to church. They really should be here because they are greatly troubled, and I know that God will meet their needs if you would just go by their house."

The problem is that this is request number 440 that the pastor has received that week. If the pastor handles all of them, he won't have time to study the Word and do his part as the pastor. What am I saying? Be like the disciples—*you* go visit your friends and relatives. Have coffee with them, tell them they need God and that they need to be in church—and then *you* bring them to church.

You tell them that you know where the answers are to their questions and that you'll come by on Sunday morning and pick them up and take them to church with you. You'll simply be telling them what the disciples told Bartimaeus, "Be of good cheer. The Master calls for you."

That may be why people don't get saved or healed in your church. Are you doing your part? If you want to see people get saved, invite unsaved people from your neighborhood, your family, or your place of work. How are they going to get there? You bring them to church. If you want to see sick people get healed (and there are probably some sick people in your church), you should go get them and bring them to church.

If you do your part and bring them to church, then the pastor can do his part; and your friends or loved ones may even end up walking down the aisle in response to the altar call. If they need to receive Jesus, they'll receive Jesus. If they need a miracle, they'll receive their miracle—all because you obeyed God's call to the ministry of helps.

BE IN YOUR OWN STORY

Do you remember Jesus' statement, "If I be lifted up, I'll draw all men unto Me"? Jesus eventually made it to the cross, but He only had a certain amount of time to get there, and He could have been late and missed it.

If Jesus had sailed in the boat by Himself, if He had passed out all the food by Himself, if He had gone to get the donkey and ride it in to Jerusalem by Himself, He would not have made it to the cross on time. I believe the reason He fulfilled His goal was because the disciples didn't develop a bad attitude, even though they had many opportunities, and they did their part. Because they operated faithfully in the ministry of helps, Jesus made it to Calvary on time.

When the Roman soldiers nailed Jesus to the cross, that cross was lying on the ground. After they nailed His hands and feet to it, they picked it up, and they dropped it into a hole, fulfilling His spoken words and Bible prophecy that when He was lifted up, He would draw all men to Him.

Jesus finished what was in His heart to do on the way to the cross because of the ministry of helps. He taught the disciples and us how to serve. Then, in dying on the cross, He became known as a servant to all. (Mark 10:33.) He is our role model, and as we serve Him by serving others, we lift Him up and people will come to Him to be saved.

Every pastor should be known as a servant to all and be able to fulfill everything that God has placed upon his heart, *and so should we*. If you are not serving in your church let this book challenge you to find your place, get involved, and do all that God wants you to do. Instead of just reading these stories, be in your own stories with God, and be part of lifting up Jesus to people in your world.

STUDY NOTES

Jesus and the Ministry of Helps, Part 2

1. Read Matthew 8:23-27. What was Jesus doing while the disciples rowed the boat across the sea?
2. Did Jesus need to rest in order to be effective in the work of the ministry? Do pastors need adequate rest in order to be effective in the work of the ministry?

Who's Rowing the Boat in Most Churches Today?

3. Who is rowing the boat in most churches today? Who is rowing the boat in your church?

4. What is God's biblical picture of how a pastor operates in the ministry?

5. What happened as a result of Jesus getting enough rest and the disciples doing their part in the ministry of helps? What happens when pastors function the way God wants them to function?

Leading the Donkey

6. Did Jesus do a lot of delegating? Give three examples that we have seen so far.

7. Why did Jesus tell His disciples to go get the donkey? Why does your pastor tell you to do certain things?

8. What would have happened if the disciples had not obeyed Jesus' instructions?

Come to Their Need

9. Read Mark 10:46-52. What did the disciples say and do to come to the blind man's need?

10. When the ministry of helps cooperates with leaders in the church, what does Jesus do?

11. What can you do to help unbelievers you know come to Jesus?

Be in Your Own Story

12. What was one of the main reasons Jesus made it to the cross on time?

13. How will your pastor be able to fulfill his vision and destiny?

8

GOD USES BOTH STARS
AND CANDLES

While writing this book, I came across another definition of the ministry of helps in the *Broadman Bible Commentary* that is going to be the focus of this chapter. It describes the plan God has for His church, and it starts off by saying, "There is no hierarchy in the gifts of God. The ministry of the Church does not rest on status, but on service."[1]

Status does not impress God. Status does not move God. The only thing that impresses and moves our God is service. So many believers think that you must have status before God will really use you and do something for you. But this quote goes on to say, "No gift that serves others is little," and it ends with a statement that is what I'm going to be focusing on: "God uses both the *stars*

---

[1] Clifton J. Allen, *The Broadman Bible Commentary*, (Nashville: Broadman Press, 1973).

and the *candles* to light His world."[2]

The term *stars* refers to those in the forefront of ministry—men and women who are called of God to be preachers and teachers of the Word, prophets, Christian artists, worship leaders, and the like. We know all the stars in the Bible—people like Noah, Moses, Esther, and Paul—but many *candles* are found in Scripture too. Jesus' own disciples are an example of candles called to help a star fulfill His vision and accomplish His goals.

Those stars and candles in the Bible are people who were human just like you and I. They didn't come from another planet, and you're going to meet two of those candles in a moment. Maybe you haven't been called to be a star in God's kingdom, but every believer can be a candle.

It is a scientific fact that the intensity of light is measured by candles (technically known as *foot-candles*).[3] When something provides illumination, the light that is measured must come from a light source. Jesus is our spiritual light source when we become born again. He told us that He is the light of the world (John 8:12; 9:5), and the apostle Paul said that we are to be reflections of His light.

Show yourselves to be blameless and guiltless, innocent and uncontaminated, children of God without blemish (faultless,

---

[2] Ibid.

[3] Based on information from *Merriam-Webster's Collegiate Dictionary,* 11th Ed., (Springfield, Massachusetts: Merriam-Webster, Inc., 2003), s.v. "foot-candle."

unrebukable) in the midst of a crooked and wicked generation [spiritually perverted and perverse], among whom you are seen as bright lights (stars or beacons [candles, author's paraphrase] shining out clearly) in the [dark] world.

Philippians 2:15,16 AMP

Jesus also told us in Matthew 5:14-16 that because we are in Him, we are the light of the world. He said that we are to let our light shine and not hide it. It just so happens that in God's overall plan, some of us are stars and some are candles, but it's the same light of His Son Jesus shining through us to disperse the darkness holding our world in its death grip.

We all know that candles can shine at any time—day or night—even during storms, which is when you bring the candles out. In a storm, you may not be able to see the stars, but candles will still shine brightly. Let's see how this relates to us spiritually.

Imagine that you are in a spiritual storm, surrounded with darkness. Suddenly there's a knock at your door. You go to the door and find out it's a candle. This person says to you, "I heard you were in a storm. I just want to bring some light into your life."

A little time goes by and there's another knock at your door. You open the door and it's another candle. This person tells you the same thing, "Heard you were in a storm and wanted to bring some light and some warmth into your life."

More time goes by and the phone rings. You answer it, and on the other end is a candle who tells you, "Heard you were in a storm and wanted to bring some light and some warmth into your life." The next thing you know, you're surrounded by candles. You're surrounded by light; you're surrounded by Jesus; and suddenly you realize the storm has departed.

Are candles starting to sound pretty important?

Every four days I'm on an airplane going somewhere in the world, and I fly quite often at night. When the pilot turns on the lights on both wings of the airplane, hundreds of thousands of "candles" are being lit. The reason is so that the pilot can land the plane in the dark. Pilots need "candles" to penetrate that darkness and see the runway in order to land the plane safely.

Think how much darkness you could penetrate with ten thousand candles lit on your left and ten thousand candles lit on your right. You could "land" the Gospel anywhere in the world. All it takes is candle power.

GOD REMEMBERS WHAT
WE DO TO HELP OTHERS

Now I'm going to introduce you to the candle I mentioned earlier. One of the first things I plan to do when I get to heaven is to go to this person, sit him down, and ask him what his name is because not only has he helped me so much over the years through his faithfulness and his commitment, but I can relate to him as a nameless person.

Many times in the past my name was not said when I was introduced in church. For instance, the pastor would tell someone, "There's our head usher," or "There's one of our nursery workers," without mentioning my name. He probably didn't realize he was doing that, but sometimes it bothered me because it implied that I was not that important.

Later, when I'd go into churches to minister, pastors would talk to me the same way about their bus captain, their outreach director, or other ministry of helps workers. Occasionally I'd ask the pastor what their names were out of respect for those people and because I'd think of the nameless candle I had discovered in the Bible.

This man appears in the book of 1 Samuel. Israel has just defeated the Philistines, but they had to regroup and come back.

> **And the Philistines gathered together to fight with Israel, 30,000 chariots, 6,000 horsemen, and people as the sand which is on the sea shore in multitude. And they came up and pitched in Michmash eastward from Bethaven. And when the men of Israel saw that they were in a strait (for the people were distressed,) then the people did hide themselves in caves, and in thickets, and in rocks, and in high places, and in pits.**

> **1 Samuel 13:5,6**

Do you ever feel like you're surrounded? Do you ever feel like there are more of your enemy than there are of you? Try to visualize this scene and how the Israelites must have felt. The Philistines had surrounded Israel with thirty thousand chariots, six thousand horsemen, and so many infantry that to count them would be like trying to count sand on the seashore. When the Israelites saw this, they panicked, ran away, and tried to hide in caves, in rocks, and in thickets. They even hid in a pit.

Have you ever been in a pit? Doing something foolish can get you into a pit, and Israel did a foolish thing. They needed tools of war, but the Philistines had made sure that not one blacksmith could be found in all of Israel. (v. 19.) It is possible that in previous wars the Philistines took away all of Israel's smiths and didn't allow any iron tools to be forged by the Philistine smiths except for farming.[4] Israel didn't try to secretly make their own weapons, and now there were only two swords left in the land—Saul had one, and his son, Jonathan, had the other.

I'm sure you've heard of Saul and Jonathan in the Bible. They are both stars. But I want to introduce you to a candle who served one of these stars faithfully. Have you ever heard of the armorbearer for Jonathan? You may feel that he can't be that important because his name isn't mentioned in the Scriptures. But God doesn't forget what we do to help others; and as we're about to see, an armorbearer was a man of resource and courage who protected his fighting companion during battles.[5] He just might have known that God

---

[4] *Adam Clarke's Commentary*, Electonic Database (copyright © 1996 by Biblesoft). All rights reserved. "1 Samuel 13:19."
[5] *International Standard Bible Encyclopedia*, Original James Orr 1915 Edition, Electronic Database (copyright © 1995-1996 by Biblesoft). All rights reserved. S.V. "Armor-Bearer."

uses both stars and candles to light His world.

COMMITTED TO WIN

Jonathan said to the young man that bear his armour, Come, and let us go over unto the garrison of these uncircumcised.

1 Samuel 14:6

Jonathan had just come up with the big idea of taking his armorbearer and one sword and going to spy out the enemy camp—an enemy who was armed with swords, spears, and bows and arrows. So he said to the young man who bore his armor, "Come on. Let's go."

What would be going through your head at that moment if you were Jonathan's armorbearer, especially when Jonathan went on to say, "It may be that the Lord will work for us"? Nothing like starting off with a little doubt! That young man was probably thinking, *I'll just smile and maybe he'll forget about it.* But then Jonathan got back into faith, saying, "There is no restraint to the Lord to save by many or by few."

Some believers might have said to Jonathan, "This is your big idea. You've got the only sword. Why don't you go on up and check it out. If everything works out okay, I'll catch up later."

How many times have pastors heard this kind of statement from church members? "You want to buy what kind of a building?" or "You want to go where and do what? Well, if and when you accomplish that, then I'll start helping in this church." When God speaks to a Jonathan and says, "Listen, there's a battle," sometimes that's when their armorbearers bail out.

Jonathan's armorbearer didn't bail out, did he? Look at what he says, "Do all that is in thine heart: Turn thee; behold, I'm with thee according to thy heart" (v. 7). What a statement of commitment. Yet, some people struggle with that statement. They think that the armorbearer was brainwashed or that he was going by blind faith.

What if we change the word *heart* to *vision?* Isn't that where the vision is, in the heart? What if the armorbearer had said, "Do all that is in thine *vision*...I'm with thee according to thy *vision*"? How important is it to have a godly vision for our lives? Proverbs 29:18 says that without a vision, we perish.

Several Bible translations of that verse refer to *vision* as revelation of God (AMP), seeing what God is doing (MSG), and divine guidance (NLT). Now can you understand why the armorbearer had no problem following a man of vision?

Let me ask you another question. Who was the armorbearer making this commitment to? This is where a lot of people make their mistake. They think that his commitment was to Jonathan, but he was not making his commitment to a man. He was making his commitment to God.

Sometimes people make a commitment to a person, and when the person stumbles and falls, they stumble and fall too. Then they wonder why. The armorbearer made his commitment to God, who never falls or fails. He recognized that the vision in Jonathan's heart came from God, and because God put it there, they could not lose!

STAND YOUR GROUND

It may have appeared that Jonathan and his armorbearer were going to get themselves killed. After all, they were outnumbered, there were only two of them, and they only had one sword. But this was a God-inspired plan, and Jonathan told his courageous companion how they were going to carry it out.

> **"Behold, we will pass over unto these men, and we will discover ourselves unto them. If they say thus unto us, Tarry until we come unto you; then we will stand still in our place, and will not go up unto them. But if they say thus, Come up unto us; then we will go up: for the Lord hath delivered them into our hand: and this shall be a sign unto us."**

> **1 Samuel 14:8-10**

Jonathan was saying, "Come on, I know where there's a battle. This is what we've got to do to get there and win." Did Jonathan's armorbearer say, "I've got to pray about this first," or did he immediately follow Jonathan?

> **"*Both* of them discovered [showed] themselves unto the garrison of the Philistines."**

> **1 Samuel 14:11**

This is where some armorbearers fall away. When the pastor tells them his vision for the church, they don't get behind him. A typical reaction could be, "Maybe we're jumping the gun here a little bit. After all, he is young, and this is his first pastorate. Maybe we need to get together more to pray before we follow him into this battle."

If that describes you, before you join hands with your fellow armorbearers for prayer, have someone read Hebrews 6:10 out loud. Then remind yourselves that God uses both the stars and the candles to light His world. Also, be aware that the enemy has evil schemes up his sleeve to make you fail and retreat.

Notice that the Philistine enemy brought up Israel's past failures, saying, "Behold, the Hebrews come forth out of the holes where they had hid themselves" (v. 11). Have you ever been reminded of your past when you were out doing something for God? That's a tactic of the enemy to stop you from finishing what God's called you to do. It didn't stop Jonathan, and it doesn't have to stop you.

> **And the men of the garrison answered Jonathan and his armourbearer, and said, Come up to us and we will shew you a thing.**
>
> 1 Samuel 14:12

Jonathan wasn't fazed by their remarks. He said to his armorbearer, "Come up after me: for the Lord hath delivered them [into our hands and] into the hands of Israel" (v.12). The armorbearer didn't have a sword in his hand, but he was still with Jonathan.

> **And Jonathan climbed up upon his hands and upon his feet *and his armourbearer after him.*
>
> 1 Samuel 14:13

Here's another point where Jonathan's armorbearer could have bailed out and run away. But I believe at that moment he reminded himself of his pledge to Jonathan at the bottom of the hill, "Do all that is within thine heart. *And behold I'm with thee according to thy heart*" (v.7). We know he kept his word because the Bible says that he climbed up on his hands and feet after Jonathan. In other words, when Jonathan stood up, he stood up. When Jonathan moved forward, he moved forward.

I've had many wonderful armorbearers over the years, but a few of them didn't toe the mark. When there was a battle to be won and I would tackle a project, instead of pitching in and helping me, they would say, "You ought to be happy I just show up." Or they'd stand there and watch without lifting a hand; and when it was over, I'd tell myself, "You did that perfectly." Most people would rather just sit there and watch. If you know someone like that, I encourage you to give them a copy of this book.

PICK UP THE SWORD

I don't know about you, but I don't want to be behind a Jonathan who goes into a battle just singing "Onward, Christian soldiers, marching onto war"[6] and walking backwards! I want to follow a Jonathan who knows how to go into a battle and how to use a sword.

---

[6] "Onward, Christian Soldier," words by Sabine Baring- Gould, music by Arthur S. Sullivan.

When Jonathan's loyal armorbearer followed him into battle, "they [the Philistines] fell before Jonathan; *and his armourbearer slew after him.* And that first slaughter, which Jonathan *and his armourbearer* made, was about twenty men" (vv. 13,14).

Now that is a puzzling passage. Initially the armorbearer didn't have a sword. Jonathan had the sword. So how did the armorbearer fight "after him"? Perhaps he stood there and cried, "Fall!" Or maybe he encouraged Jonathan, saying, "They don't like us. They laughed at us. You've got the sword of the Lord; make them fall before you. There's a soldier, right there, Jonathan. Here's another soldier, over here. Go get them, Jonathan!" But I'm sure that's not what happened.

This armorbearer was right behind Jonathan, and I believe that he stumbled upon a dead soldier who had a sword. He wasn't using it anymore, so the armorbearer picked it up, and now there were two swords in the battle. But there would not have been two swords in the battle if the armorbearer had said, "This is your project, Jonathan. You've got the only sword. Why don't you go on and check it out. If everything works out okay, then I'll catch up later."

Many people feel that their pastor is the only one who really knows how to use the sword. Of course, I'm not talking about a real sword. One way the Bible uses the term *sword* is to symbolize the Word of God. (Eph. 6:7; Heb. 4:12.) We use the sword of the Word in spiritual battles to defeat the devil by speaking it out loud when we pray for ourselves and others. Another way we use the sword is by tackling a project—just showing up, pitching in, and helping the pastor.

If the armorbearers would just show up for the battle, if they would just try to defeat the first obstacle the enemy puts in their way, they would realize that it works, and they would pick up their swords every time. Then there would be at least two swords in the battle. Imagine what the church could accomplish then!

Look what happened when Jonathan and his armorbearer went into battle together. God used a star and a candle, and they were dropping the Philistines left and right.

> And that first slaughter, which Jonathan and his armourbearer made, was about twenty men, within as it were an half acre of land, which a yoke of oxen might plow. And there was trembling in the host, in the field, and among all the people: the garrison, and the spoilers, they also trembled, and the earth quaked: so it was a very great trembling.

> 1 Samuel 14:14,15

That word *slaughter* tells me that Jonathan didn't come into the enemy camp and politely ask if anyone wanted to swordfight. He came in swinging his sword so forcefully that it caused "a very great trembling" on the earth.

Perhaps it was inconceivable to the Philistines that only two Hebrew men would attack them, so they were terrified at the thought that there must be a larger force of Israelites just over the rocky slope. The sudden shock of the attack, aided by an earthquake, caused the Philistines to tremble with panic and become so confused that they began "swinging their [own] swords wildly, killing each other" (v. 20 MSG).

The whole mission was begun and carried out by the faith of a star and a candle, but it was born of God who gave them the victory when they worked together to accomplish His will. That's what it is going to take to spread the light of Jesus and penetrate the darkness in the world. It is going to take the stars and the candles *working together.*

GOD ALSO USES WOMEN

In Acts 9:36-43, the Bible tells us about the life and ministry of a woman named Tabitha, who is also called Dorcas. I'll never forget the first time I read this passage about her. I had a poor image of women because of how I was raised on the farm and how I had been taught. All I saw women do in our family was cook, sew, clean house, and have babies. And the teacher of the first Bible study I attended was a man who said that the Bible says women are to be quiet in church. They are never to stand before a group of people and teach the Word of God. He wasn't married, and I think he had a problem with women in ministry.

I'll never forget the first class I had when I got to Bible school because it was on women in the Bible. The teacher said that God uses women in ministry. I thought, *Man, we just got them under control, and now you say God wants to use them!* Obviously, I was a little confused at that time.

When I read about Dorcas in the book of Acts, I wondered why the Bible was talking about her. She didn't do anything that great, like preaching or healing the sick. She just did "good works and almsdeeds" (Acts 9:36). To me, that sounded just like the women where I grew up. It certainly didn't sound like she was a minister. Then she got sick and died. Other believers washed her and prepared her for burial, and she went to heaven (Buddy Bell translation), but it seems God wasn't done with her. Her friends went to get Peter.

Dorcas's friends showed Peter the coats and garments she had made. At that point I'm thinking, *Did she do that much to justify Peter coming to her?* But God uses both the stars and the candles to light His world. It says Peter told everyone to leave, and he kneeled down and prayed. What did Peter pray? Some say he prayed a great prayer of faith. Some say he asked God to heal her. But I believe his prayer might have sounded a little like Hebrews 6:10.

"God, You are not an unrighteous God. You will not forget our work and labor of love. And Tabitha has put forth a lot of work and labor of love. Hear, oh God." Then he turned to the body and said, "Tabitha, arise." She opened her eyes, took Peter's hand, and he presented her to the friends who loved her so much (Acts 9:40,41.)

The Bible goes on to say that many believed in the Lord that day because a candle was raised from the dead—a female candle. This was the first time I saw that God does use both the stars and the candles—and both men and women—to light His world! It was reading this story of Dorcas that caused my entire view of women and ministry to begin to change.

As I continued to study women in the Bible, I found other examples where they served in the ministry of helps, such as the woman who washed Jesus' feet in Luke 7:37-50. The religious people criticized Jesus for allowing her to touch Him because she was a sinner. But Jesus saw her heart, that she loved Him and worshipped Him. He forgave her and corrected the religious people by telling them, "Wherefore I say unto thee, her sins, which are many, are forgiven; for she loved much: but to whom little is forgiven, the same loveth little." Jesus used this woman in the ministry of helps to illustrate love and forgiveness.

Mary of Bethany, the sister of Martha and Lazarus, also anointed Jesus. This is a very interesting passage of Scripture because it also shows the corruption that was already working in Judas's heart.

Then took Mary a pound of ointment of spikenard, very costly, and anointed the feet of Jesus, and wiped his feet with her hair: and the house was filled with the odour of the ointment.

Then saith one of his disciples, Judas Iscariot, Simon's son, which should betray him,

Why was not this ointment sold for three hundred pence, and given to the poor?

This he said, not that he cared for the poor; but because he was a thief, and had the bag, and bare what was put therein.

Then said Jesus, Let her alone: against the day of my burying hath she kept this.

For the poor always ye have with you; but me ye have not always.

John 12:3-8

The contrast between Judas and Mary really hit me. Judas was a thief who didn't care about the people; and the Bible says in 1 John 4:20 that if you don't love your brother, then you don't love God. He was one of Jesus' disciples, a man who was a leader in Jesus' ministry. Yet Mary, a woman, loved Jesus, loved the people, and was the only one who understood He was soon going to die. So she was anointing Him for death. In other words, a woman who operated in the ministry of helps loved Him and served Him better than a man who was on His leadership team.

I also noticed that Judas criticized Mary for anointing Jesus with very expensive oil. In the ministry of helps, we worship and serve Jesus by serving His body of believers, and sometimes we are criticized because we do so much for them or spend so much time and money on "little things." An example I have already mentioned is picking up our pastor and driving him to church and back so that he can stay focused on the message God has given him.

Don't misunderstand me. I'm not saying a pastor should live in a mansion and drive a Mercedes™ when his entire congregation can barely keep food on the table and clothes on their backs. But we should honor the men and women of God who serve us as we would honor Jesus Himself. I think women understand this better than men do because they tend to be more submissive and are taught from an early age to serve others. They also are more emotional, which is not always a bad thing! They can "get a clue" to what's really going on when men are scratching their heads trying to figure out what's happening in a certain situation.

Women are also extremely courageous in the way they love. If you've ever seen a wife "stand by her man" or a mother protect her children from someone or something that is trying to hurt them, you know what I mean! The women loved Jesus so much that they stayed at the cross when all the men but John ran away in fear of their own lives. (Matt. 27:55,56; John 19:25-27.) And the Bible says that they ministered to Jesus. They even prepared His body for burial, which is another great example of women in the ministry of helps. (Luke 23:55,56.)

After Jesus was resurrected and the church was born at Pentecost, women continued to play a big role in ministry. We've already seen how important Dorcas was in Acts 9. In Acts 18:1-3, Priscilla worked in the ministry with her husband, Acquila, and the apostle Paul. Paul mentions her in both his letter to the Romans and his first letter to the Corinthians. In Acts 18:24-26, with her husband, Priscilla taught Apollos "the more excellent way." So we see that women in the New Testament not only teach, but they teach men!

Then I read about the four daughters of Philip the Evangelist in Acts 21:8-9. All of them prophesied in the church. Many believers and leaders in the body of Christ today believe that the Bible says that women should be silent in church, but I believe that this comes from wrong teaching of a few verses of Scripture taken out of context. There are many great books on this subject that you can read to study this out for yourself, such as *The Woman Question* by Kenneth Hagin, Sr. But what really changed my mind about this was when the Holy Spirit opened my eyes to see all the women in the New Testament who ministered in various gifts and callings, especially in the ministry of helps. Women can be stars as well as candles.

From the time we were married, my wife has always been my partner in ministry. She has gifts and insight and abilities that I don't have, so we complement each other. She is as valuable and powerful a minister as any man I know. So not only did God show me in His Word that women were ministers, but He showed me through my wife. There is no doubt in my mind and heart that God uses women as well as men in the ministry, and women are especially great in the ministry of helps because they have such love and understanding for other people's needs.

WHO IS IMPORTANT?

There is one last thing I want you to think about. There were no stars raised from the dead in the Bible. I often tell zealous Christians wanting to be stars that if they happen to die before their time, they probably won't be back! On the other hand, if they are a candle and something happens to them, there's a good chance they will be raised from the dead like Dorcas was.

The Bible says in 1 Corinthians 12:18 that God puts the members of the body of Christ where He wants them and uses them as He sees fit. It also says in verses 21-25 that every member is equally important, that we should honor and love every member the same, whether they are an apostle or a greeter at the door.

We must always remember that both the apostle and the greeter are anointed by God to lead people to Jesus, heal the sick, cast out demons, feed the poor, and clothe the naked. God picks the stars and the candles to light His world, and when our churches come in to agreement with Him, they can accomplish so much more.

STUDY NOTES

God Uses Both Stars and Candles
1. "The ministry of the Church does not rest on _____

but on _____." What does not impress God? What does impress God? Do you need to change your mind about what impresses you?

2. Read Philippians 2:15-16 and Matthew 5:14-16. Only some believers are called to be stars, but all of us are called to be candles. How can you let your light shine in your world?

3. Where do we find light in a storm? How does a pilot land a plane when it is dark outside?

God Remembers What We Do to Help Others

4. Who are often the "nameless" believers in the church?

5. What is an armorbearer?

Committed to Win

6. When do armorbearers usually bail out?

7. Read Proverbs 29:18. What must a leader have in order for believers, and especially armorbearers, to follow and be committed?

8. Who are armorbearers and believers committed to? In other words, whose vision do they follow?

Stand Your Ground

9. Again, when do armorbearers usually fall away? What does the enemy do to try to get us to fall away?

10. What weapons did Jonathan's armorbearer have when he followed Jonathan into battle?

11. What did Jonathan's armorbearer do when Jonathan began to climb up on his hands and knees?

Pick Up the Sword

12. How did Jonathan's armorbearer fight "after him"?

13. What is our "sword"? Who is qualified to use the sword? In what ways do we use the sword?

14. Read 1 Samuel 14:14-16. What happens when both stars and candles work together?

God Also Uses Women

15. Read Acts 9:36-43. What did Tabitha do that caused the other believers to love her so much and the apostle Peter to raise her from the dead?

16. Read Luke 7:37-50. What truth was illustrated when this woman washed Jesus' feet?

17. Read John 12:3-8 and 19:25-27. How were women instrumental in Jesus accomplishing His purpose?

18. Discuss how the emotions of women can enhance their ability to minister and worship.

19. Name three women in the New Testament who ministered either as stars or candles and tell what each did to further the Gospel.

Who Is Important?

20. How many stars were raised from the dead in the Bible (not counting Jesus)?

21. Read 1 Corinthians 12:18, 21-25. What is every believer anointed to do, regardless of status or position?

22. Who is most important in the body of Christ, and who is not that important?

9

PREREQUISITE FOR A
VICTORIOUS MINISTRY

Not slothful in business; fervent in spirit; serving the Lord.

Romans 12:11

Several years ago, I came to a place in my life and in my Christian walk where confusion began to interfere with my progress. The confusion was in the area of zeal. I noticed that a lot of people did not understand zeal. Some Christians acted as if zeal were a disease.

In Romans 12:11, the word *fervent* means "zealous": So the Bible says that we need to have zeal in serving the Lord.

But many times Christians would tell me I was full of zeal, and then they would back up as if I had something they did not want. You say *zeal* in some churches, and it is as if you said a dirty word.

When I began to look into this subject, however, I discovered a lot of people do not know what zeal is. They think *zeal* means bouncing off the walls and rolling on the floor. That is not zeal.

I know other Christians who seem to pick and choose what parts of God they want. But how can you pick and choose? I want *all* of God.

Then, I heard a preacher say that the zeal of God is like a consuming fire. I know that nothing can stand against the fire of God, and I know that the devil will try to put this and that on me. But if I stay full of the zeal of God, those things cannot stay on me. Nothing can stand against the fire of God.

I have watched congregations sing about the zeal of God coming over them and burning in their souls, but you could see from their faces they were just singing words. They had no revelation of the words they were singing. In my visits to churches, the most people I have found in one place who understood the zeal of God was six.

One day, I decided to find out what the Bible says about zeal. I believe it is time for Christians to take zeal out of their spiritual closets, shake the dust off it, and apply it in their lives.

WHAT DOES THE BIBLE SAY ABOUT ZEAL?

For he put on righteousness as a breastplate, and an helmet of salvation upon his head; and he put on the garments of vengeance for clothing, and was clad with zeal as a cloak.

Isaiah 59:17

That verse is part of a prophecy about Jesus, and the prophet said that the Messiah would put on zeal like a coat. He would cover Himself with zeal. Did Jesus not know it was wrong to have zeal? Did He not know He would be considered a second-class citizen if He walked around in zeal?

After reading just that one verse, I wondered where people got the idea that zeal was something suspicious and undesirable.

Psalm 119:139 says:

My zeal hath consumed me, because mine enemies have forgotten thy words.

How many of us today could stand up and say our zeal for the cause of Christ has consumed us?

Look at Isaiah 9:6-7:

For unto us a child is born, unto us a son is given: and the government shall be upon his shoulder: and his name shall be called Wonderful, Counsellor, The mighty God, The everlasting Father, The Prince of Peace.

Of the increase of his government and peace there shall be no end, upon the throne of David, and upon his kingdom, to order it, and to establish it with judgment and with justice from henceforth even for ever. The zeal of the Lord of hosts will perform this.

Do you want the government to be established on the shoulders of Jesus Christ? I do. Some inroads have been made into turning our government around, but there is something missing. The last part of that verse says that the zeal of the Lord will perform this.

That is what is missing today—the zeal of the Lord of hosts. Why do we back away from it in the church?

Isaiah 63:15 should be the prayer of the church:

> Look down from heaven, and behold from the habitation of thy holiness and of thy glory: where is thy zeal and thy strength, the sounding of thy bowels and of thy mercies toward me? are they restrained?

Where is the zeal of God in the church today? Nobody knows, and some are glad it is not around.

WHY ARE WE AFRAID OF ZEAL?

Why is the body of Christ afraid of the zeal of God? Perhaps we ought to look at some verses that have been used to throw zeal out of the church.

> Brethren, my heart's desire and prayer to God for Israel is, that they might be saved.
>
> For I bear them record that they have a zeal of God, but not according to knowledge.
>
> For they being ignorant of God's righteousness, and going about to establish their own righteousness, have not submitted themselves unto the righteousness of God.
>
> Romans 10:1-3

Did Paul write that it is wrong to have zeal?

Did he write that all Christians need to get rid of zeal, that all we need is knowledge?

Misunderstanding those verses is one reason Christians say, "You're just full of zeal. You need the Word of God."

What Paul was saying is this: "My brethren have a zeal toward God, but they do not have the right knowledge to base that on. They are trying to work out the zeal of God in their own righteousness instead of in His."

Their knowledge is what was wrong, not their zeal. In earlier church times, we had the zeal, but somewhere along the way, Christians decided it was time to put zeal aside and get hold of the Word of God. Get knowledge! Now, in all the "knowledge", people are sitting around saying something is missing. They have been getting hold of the Word of God for years, and there is still something missing.

Paul did not say to get rid of one and go after the other. What would happen if we put zeal and knowledge together?

Remember when you got saved? Remember when you first were a Christian? You could not wait for the church doors to open. You were on fire. You were hot. Then along came Brother and Sister Knowledge, and you began to grow cold.

I was out driving in Tulsa, Oklahoma, near our home once with my four daughters, when one of them yelled, "Daddy, look at that flag. Look how big it is! It's an American flag too!"

I looked, and I noticed that the flag was just hanging there. It was not doing anything. God does not want us to let our zeal "flag," waiting for some circumstance, some outside influence, to come along and blow on it.

Are you just hanging there? What about when the wind comes up? Do not be satisfied just to be a "flag" for God. You are in control. Maintain your spiritual glow. Zeal is not some weird thing that might get on you. Zeal means serving the Lord with an energetic spirit; some translations say to keep the fires of the spirit burning.

WHO KEEPS ZEAL INTACT?

All of that sounds as if it is our responsibility to keep the zeal of God intact and alive in us.

> Epaphras, who is one of you, a servant of Christ, saluteth you, always labouring fervently for you in prayers, that ye may stand perfect and complete in all the will of God.
>
> For I bear him record, that he hath a great zeal for you, and them that are in Laodicea, and them in Hierapolis.
>
> Colossians 4:12,13

Where do people come up with this teaching that it is wrong to have zeal? Where do they get this idea that zeal is a part of God you really do not want?

> Looking for that blessed hope, and the glorious appearing of the great God and our Saviour Jesus Christ;
>
> Who gave himself for us, that he might redeem us from all iniquity, and purify unto himself a peculiar people, zealous of good works.
>
> Titus 2:13,14

Are you part of a peculiar people? Jesus is coming after a peculiar people zealous of good works. Can you imagine a big bus that comes down from heaven, the door opens, and out steps an angel who says:

"May I have your attention please? Would all of you who are just peculiar please step to the left? Now, you who are peculiar and zealous of good works, I would like for you to get on, and we'll take right off. You that are just peculiar, we might be back."

I was preaching this in one church, and just as I came to the part about the bus, a bus pulled up outside. Some of the people broke out in a sweat! You could see them thinking, *Hurry up and tell us, Brother Bell! What is it? The bus has arrived!* Well, we have some time yet before this bus arrives.

Look at what Jesus said in Revelation 3:19:

> As many as I love, I rebuke and chasten: be zealous therefore, and repent.

Did Jesus not know that *zeal* is a "no-no"? For almost ten years, I have been in hundreds of churches, and I have noticed something.

Not only is there little zeal; there is very little repentance going on.

You say, "I don't have to come forward to repent. God meets me at my chair."

But when you repent, you turn 180 degrees and go the other way. Genuine repentance brings change. But people do not come to the altar anymore. Sometimes, churches do not even have altars. I have heard people say that years ago, the altars were always full. Christians were on their knees repenting. People are not repenting today because there is little zeal in the church. Many Christians do not know what the zeal of God is.

When I got to this place in my study of zeal, I made up my mind and said in my heart that Buddy Bell would never again deny the zeal of God. It was settled in my heart that I would never stand still and be quiet when a Christian pointed out other Christians and criticized their zeal. Yet I could not tell you what zeal was.

ZEAL IN A NUTSHELL

One day as I was riding in the backseat of a car headed for a meeting, I was thinking about zeal. I was not ready to teach on it yet because I did not have a full understanding. But I was meditating on these Scriptures and definitions.

And I said, "Lord, would You just put it in a nutshell for me? What is Your zeal?"

The Lord said, "Buddy, My zeal is a never-quitting attitude." Jesus surrounded Himself with a never-quitting attitude.

The Word of God says that the government would be established on the shoulders of Jesus by a never-quitting attitude in the body of Christ. We cannot quit! We need to be able to say that we are consumed by a never-quitting attitude.

Jesus is coming for a peculiar people, a people with a never-quitting attitude toward good works. Allow the zeal of God to come up on the inside of you. Do not quit.

When I began to travel and hold seminars in churches and auditoriums, something began to happen that, at first, I would not tell anyone for fear they would think I had flipped out. If a meeting did not go quite right, I would go back to the motel, look at myself in the mirror, and say:

"Buddy Bell, get it together. You are going to do what God wants you to do. You are going to go where God wants you to go. You are going to be what God wants you to be. You are not going to quit."

After I did this study on zeal, I realized it was the zeal of God rising up inside me that caused me to do that. That was zeal rising up to consume me. When I am consumed with that never-quitting attitude, there is nothing the devil can throw at me to stop me.

You need knowledge, but do not throw away the zeal. Without

zeal, knowledge will not be of much value. Catch hold of the zeal of God, and your helps ministry will be victorious. Have a zeal for what God has set you to do, and it will be easy to be obedient and faithful in it. You cannot fulfill your calling in the helps ministry without zeal.

10

"THEY'D HAVE TO PAY ME
TO GO IN THERE!"

What would cause a first-time visitor to want to come back to your church? Experts say that a family will determine in the first six minutes after driving on to your church property if they will return or not. As I pondered that one time, I thought about the story of the Queen of Sheba and her first visit to King Solomon's palace. I ended up drawing some spiritual parallels. What you're about to see in these next three chapters may surprise you because one of the first things that profoundly impressed her was the ministry of helps.

The Queen of Sheba was a monarch from a distant land, who made a great journey to see for herself if all that she had heard about the legendary Hebrew ruler was true.

When the queen of Sheba heard of the fame of Solomon,
she came to prove Solomon with hard questions at Jerusalem,

with a very great company, and camels that bare spices, and gold in abundance, and precious stones: and when she was come to Solomon, she communed with him of all that was in her heart. And Solomon told her all her questions: and there was nothing hid from Solomon which he told her not.

2 Chronicles 9:1,2

Can you tell that this woman was rich? She carried her jewels and precious stones on camels. Most women would love to have just one camel loaded down with jewels and precious stones. A little later on you'll see why this is significant.

And when the queen of Sheba had seen....

2 Chronicles 9:3

I want to focus on the word *seen* or *sight* in this verse. I realize that believers are not supposed to be moved by what we see, or by what we hear, smell, taste, or feel. But if we're not supposed to use our senses, why did God give them to us? He equipped us with natural senses because we live in the natural world. However, we are not to allow ourselves to be controlled by them.

Consider this scenario. If my nose (sense of smell) isn't working when I pick up a glass of sour milk, and my tongue (sense of taste) isn't working; if I drink some of that sour milk, my stomach will work. I'll soon feel the effects of drinking the sour milk, but it won't be a pleasant experience. And I won't want more of it!

In the same way, first-time church visitors are moved by their senses, beginning with what they see (sense of sight). I've driven by some churches, and just by seeing them from the outside I've thought, *They'd have to pay me to go in there—and many have.* The ministry of helps has the responsibility to keep that from being the first impression of their church.

WISDOM CAN BE SEEN

When the queen of Sheba had seen the wisdom of Solomon, and the house that he had built.

2 Chronicles 9:3

God made Solomon's wisdom so great that his reputation echoed throughout the known world, even into the palaces of kings and queens. The Queen of Sheba had heard of the wisdom of Solomon and had gone to great trouble and expense to see it for herself—and she wasn't disappointed. It was the first thing she noticed.

Wisdom can be seen in the way things function, the way things are handled, the way things are managed and taken care of. Solomon's wisdom was seen throughout the house he had built, which was the second thing the Queen of Sheba noticed. Churches are often referred to as the house of God, and their appearance should reflect that because visitors see the church's exterior before they ever see the interior. This is one time when the outward appearance is very important.

In this passage, I thought it was interesting that a woman would notice a building, but they do notice buildings. They notice the décor of buildings on the outside and on the inside—and it affects them in a different way than it affects men. Women like certain color schemes. They like to see plants and flowers and church banners. Generally, men don't notice exterior or interior decorations. Most men are not affected by their surroundings. Just give them a block of cement to stand on, and they'll preach. Give them a chair to sit on, and they'll listen to the Word.

Recently, I was with a pastor friend of mine who has a fairly large church in Chicago, Illinois, and he said something about this that really made sense. "Would you agree that there are more women than there are men in the majority of the congregations you have ministered to?" I agreed with him.

Then he said, "Think about the church buildings you've preached in. Wouldn't you agree that the majority of those church buildings—on the outside as well as on the inside—have a very cold look and feel to them?" Again, I had to agree.

My pastor friend continued, "If you're not relaxed, if you're not comfortable and at ease, if you don't have peace in church, the odds are that you're not going to bring someone else into that same atmosphere." That is so true.

Churches need to put some life on the outside of their buildings. Plant some flowers and other greenery, and have a well-kept lawn.

Then, when people drive by they will think, *If there's life on the outside, there might be life on the inside.*

When we sold our home, our realtor said to put any extra money we had on the outside of the house. If people drove by and didn't like the outside, the odds were that they wouldn't pick up the phone to find out what was on the inside. I know that sounds extreme, but the next time you go to church, take a close look at the churches you pass by on the way to yours. The church that receives the care and attention to detail is the one people will decide to visit.

GOT LIFE?

Have you noticed over the years how gas stations have evolved? They've gone through an extreme makeover—from the plain, drab look of having just two pumps sticking out of the ground and no inviting décor to a spruced-up front area with plants and shrubs and great lighting. That way, even if you drive in there late at night, it looks like daytime.

I was told by some gas station owners that oil companies have actually done expensive studies to find out how to attract women as customers because so many women today are driving vehicles and pumping their own gas. They found that if they planted a few flowers out front, the odds are that women will pull into their gas station instead of the one across the street that's only got two pumps sticking out of the ground, car parts lying around everywhere, and a gas station attendant dressed in coveralls, who is chewing and spitting tobacco. Their study showed that women will even pay two to three cents more a gallon to go to a landscaped gas station.

The point is, when visitors drive on to the church property, the first few minutes will determine whether or not they will return to that church. Landscaping plays a big role in their decision. What do visitors see when they first arrive at your church?

One time I went to speak at a church that was way out in the country. The pastor was very excited because they had just built a new building. But what really excited him was the fact that they had a paved parking lot. That was really something for a church in "the back forty."

The pastor wanted me to see that paved parking lot more than he wanted me to see his building. We drove out there, and as we came around the last curve, I was stunned. He had a concrete parking lot all right—it was concrete right up to the four walls of that church. Not one blade of grass, one flower, one tree, or one shrub was on that whole property! It looked like a funeral home.

My first thought was that he didn't have any women on his building committee. When I mentioned that to him, he looked at me in astonishment and said, "How did you know?" I said, "There's no grass or flowers or trees or shrubs anywhere in sight!"

"I know," he said. "We did that on purpose. We're tired of cutting the grass around here. We're tired of planting flowers and trimming the shrubs." He had left out what adds life on the outside of a church and makes people want to knock down the doors to get in.

PUT YOUR BEST FOOT FORWARD

Here's something I hear quite often in my travels to different churches: "Why don't more intelligent people come to our church?" I'm not sure how they define "intelligent people," but one reason more people in general don't come could be that what they see first on the outside is what they believe they will continue to see if they go inside.

Something that can really make a bad first impression is the sign out in front of a church. I've preached in some churches that have a sign out front that words can be put on, but letters are missing because there aren't enough to finish spelling a word. In some cases, the words aren't even abbreviated the right way. I've actually had well-intentioned leaders tell me they are believing God that everyone who passes by will know what they mean.

Don't put anything up on a church sign if you run out of letters! And be sure the words are spelled correctly. When people drive by and see a sign with misspelled words on it, they think there aren't any intelligent people on the inside, and they'll make a mental note to stay away.

Something else to be careful of are church flagpoles. An empty flagpole gives the message that there must not be anybody around. A flag should be flying from that flagpole, and it should not be a flag that is faded, ripped, or torn. If yours is, get a new one. When people see the same old faded, ripped, torn flag every time they drive by, it gives them the feeling that nobody cares in that church.

It's human nature to judge the interior by the exterior, whether it's people or buildings or some other entity. Boosting church growth may begin as simply as taking a closer look at the outside of your church.

CLEANLINESS IS PART OF GODLINESS

Once visitors enter the church building, often the first place they go is to your bathroom. I know some women who will only buy gas from gas stations that have the cleanest and nicest bathrooms. People tend to have a similar philosophy for churches. The bathroom will determine if they're going to come back or not, so it had better be clean.

I'll never forget the time I was invited to preach in a church, and someone from the church came to my hotel to pick me up. I had to use the restroom, but they had already arrived to get me; so I thought I'd wait until I got to the church. This church was only a couple of years old, but when I walked in there, I couldn't believe what I saw. It was one of the filthiest churches I've ever been in. The bathroom was so dirty that when I went inside, I did not use it. I turned around and walked back out.

When it was time for me to preach, I preached a short, twenty-minute message, said "Amen," and left, not because I was mad but because *I had to use the bathroom!* I had to go someplace else to find one that was clean. Surely first-time visitors to a church in that condition will feel the same way.

SERVINGS OF MEAT

Another thing the Queen of Sheba noticed was the meat on Solomon's table.

And the meat of his table....

2 Chronicles 9:4

The word *meat* is referring to food that nourishes the physical body. Solomon obviously served the choicest meat—perhaps prime rib, filet mignon, or tenderloin. But in the Bible, meat can also refer to spiritual food that "sustains and nourishes spiritual life or holiness."[1]

Have you ever had anybody ask you what your pastor preaches on Sunday morning? People who ask that kind of question are usually looking for a pastor who preaches a message with some spiritual meat to it. Possibly the church they've been attending is just feeding them the milk of the Word. After a while, as we begin

---

[1] Noah Webster, s.v. "MEAT."

to grow in the Lord, milk just doesn't satisfy anymore. (Heb. 5:12-14.) We need to be fed the meat of the Word because that's what makes us become mature sons and daughters of God.

Telling people about the "steak" that your pastor serves on Sundays and Wednesdays won't scare them away. If you just tell people a little milk dish portion of a powerful sermon your pastor preached one time, it is no wonder they don't come to your church.

I believe there was more on Solomon's table than just pieces of meat, but the meat is what grabbed the Queen's attention. If someone you know is looking for a church that feeds them the meat of the Word, tell them what's being served at your church. "If you want steak, you need to come on Sunday morning—we have steak on Sunday mornings and Sunday nights, and prime rib on Wednesday nights!"

"BRING OUT THE FAITH CHAIRS"

It's a biblical fact that first-time visitors notice how many people come to church.

"When the Queen of Sheba had seen...the sitting of his servants."

2 Chronicles 9:4

Remember, the Queen of Sheba was a first-time visitor to Israel. How do visitors know the number of people who don't come to a church if this is their first visit? Every chair in the auditorium—

empty or filled—represents a person.

You might disagree with me on this, but I think it's pretty safe to say that the main reason that 99.9 percent of visitors visit a church is out of curiosity. By telling people great things about your church, you can peak their interest.

Some Christians say that it's hard to get people to come to their church. When I hear people say that, it tells me they don't talk about their church outside of the four walls of that church. All you have to do is talk about your church. You don't have to preach to people, just tell them what goes on there. Tell them how your pastor is a wild, powerful, anointed preacher. Tell them about your tremendous children's ministry. Tell them about your fantastic youth ministry that is reaching so many young people for Christ.

Everybody has a different curiosity level, and when theirs gets to a certain point—maybe the 110th time you ask them to come—they'll say, "You know what? I want to come. I want to go down there and see that for myself."

Maybe you've told them that Jesus lives in your church, that God lives there, that the Holy Ghost lives there, that the pastor walks on water and his wife's an angel—she's got wings! But if, when they walk into the church, they see half of the chairs empty, their first thought is probably going to be, *If this church is so wonderful, where is everybody?*

You may tell them, "Oh, we're all here," but they'll say, "No, you're not. Where are all *those* people?" as they point to the empty seats in the auditorium. Empty chairs do not impress people.

I often call pastors of churches where I'm going to preach to find out a little bit beforehand about their church. Many of them will tell me the number of people they have, saying something like, "We run about 300, but we can seat 750 people in our church." They're trying to impress me with the larger number, but they're actually saying that they can't get over 300 people to come to their church. *Empty chairs are not impressive.*

I've gone to churches that have a hundred people in attendance on Sunday morning, but their auditorium will hold 500 chairs. So, in faith they go out and buy 400 extra chairs and put them out in the auditorium. *I* understand what they're doing, and *they* understand what they're doing, but new people don't see anything but a lot of empty chairs. Again, they may have been told many wonderful things about the church, but if they walk in and see that 400 people didn't show up, they're going to doubt what they've heard. What those pastors need to do is put those 400 faith chairs in a faith room. Then when more people show up, go to that faith room and bring out some faith chairs for them to sit on.

Do you want to create some excitement in your church? Bring in chairs. It's a better report to be able to say, "This morning, we had to bring twenty extra chairs in our church. I'm telling you, God is moving." Even though you had room for 150 chairs, you just didn't put them out until you needed them. That will create excitement. What am I saying? Go ahead and buy extra chairs; just don't put them out until they're needed.

One time I came back from a meeting and my wife, Kathy, asked me how it went. I said, "The place was packed out. It was full!"

She said, "Didn't only twenty-five people show up?"

I said, "No, there were twenty-six." That may not sound like much, but that place had twenty-six chairs and twenty-six people attended, so the place was full. It was packed out.

While speaking to a group of pastors after a conference, I commended them that in every service all the seats were filled—500, to be exact. They agreed most wholeheartedly. Then I told them that the auditorium would hold 1000 chairs. I asked them if the meetings would have been as exciting in a half-empty auditorium. They saw the wisdom in setting up only the number of chairs for the number of people attending.

Wouldn't you like to have a first-time visitor leave your church after the service and say, "I went to that church, and I had to wait until they got me a chair. That auditorium was full!" instead of saying, "I went to that church and there were so few people there that I could pick any chair I wanted."

WHAT MAKES OR BREAKS A CHURCH?

Empty chairs often reflect a lack of church growth. Pastors typically get the blame when churches aren't growing or people don't come back, but they are not usually the reason. It's a proven fact that the first person you meet in a new location is going to be what influences you the most on whether or not you return.

Who do church visitors see first, the pastor or those in the ministry of helps? It's sad, but in some churches it's old Brother Fred, who is telling them where to park their car. He used to usher in the main auditorium, but he was a little rough with people, so they moved him to the parking lot team. Now the first thing a visitor hears is, "Make sure you park between the lines, and don't ask me any questions about where something is in the church." Sad, but true!

Who do your people meet first?

Remember, the pastor does not make or break a church; we, together, make or break the church.

WINNING FIRST-TIME VISITORS
STUDY NOTES

"They'd Have to Pay Me to Go in There!"

1. When do first-time visitors usually determine whether or not they will return to a church?

140

2. Why did God give you your five senses? Give an example of
    how you are to use them.

Wisdom Can Be Seen

3. How is wisdom seen?
4. Why is the outward appearance of a church important?

Got Life?

5. Explain why gas companies changed the outward appearance
    of their gas stations.
6. What does landscaping do for a church?

Put Your Best Foot Forward

7. Explain why a church's sign can either drive a prospective
    visitor away or make them want to come inside. What can it
    say to people passing by?
8. If your church has a flagpole, what are some things you should
    remember? What can this say to people passing by?

Cleanliness Is Part of Godliness

9. How important is the condition of the bathrooms in your
    church?

Servings of Meat

10. What is "spiritual meat"?
11. Why do believers need spiritual meat?

"Bring Out the Faith Chairs"

12. What does a chair in your church represent?

13. What is the best way to get someone to come to your church (other than just asking them)?

14. How do you talk about your church to the people in your life?

Do You Talk About Your Church at All?

15. What impression do a lot of empty chairs make? What happens when you don't have enough chairs and have to bring out more?

16. What can happen when you tell someone how great your church is, they finally come to visit, and there are a lot of empty chairs?

What Makes or Breaks a Church?

17. Who is the person who most often influences whether or not a visitor will return to a church?

18. Who do visitors to your church encounter first?

11

IT'S A PACKAGE DEAL: LEADERSHIP AND BEING A GODLY EXAMPLE

The "president" of the last "club" we're all going to try to join makes a special announcement before we can enter. Some church members think it goes something like this: "Well done! The one who was thinking about getting involved with the church, but couldn't quite come up with any extra time to do it." No, that's not it. A few of them think it's, "Well done! The one who would have become involved in church but didn't quite go along with everything the pastor preached and taught from the pulpit." That's not it either.

Then there's those who think it's, "Well done! The one who served in the church but didn't feel it was necessary to serve with faithfulness and integrity." But they won't be getting in either.

The truth is, in that day, when the Lord returns, He is going to announce to those who are serving faithfully, "Well done, thou *good and faithful* servant...enter thou into the joy of thy Lord" (Matt. 25:21). The last club we will all want to get into is the Faithfulness Club. I don't know about you, but I want to be serving faithfully when Jesus comes back. (v. 31.) So in this chapter we're going to see what it takes to be a faithful servant.

When we are serving faithfully, it shows. The Queen of Sheba not only noticed the sitting of Solomon's servants, she noticed "the attendance of his ministers" (2 Chron. 9:4). I'm going to make two statements about that verse.

First, *people never go beyond their leadership.* However the leadership is in the church, that's the way the people will be. I'm not just talking about pastors and their spouses. I'm talking about elders, deacons, and anyone else in a leadership position. If they're not faithful, committed, and excited about the pastor's vision for the church, I can guarantee you that the people who are under them won't be either.

Second, *if anyone should be in the church services and the meetings, the leaders in the church should be there.* Only two excuses are acceptable for leaders to miss a service or meeting.

The leader has a job in addition to serving the church.

The leader died.

The first excuse is understandable if that person has a family to support, and the second excuse is self-explanatory! Other than these reasons, leaders need to show the congregation that they are solidly behind their pastor. It's not hard to figure out why only half of the church is behind the pastor when only half of the church leaders are behind the pastor.

When I first got into the ministry and started traveling, I was told that 85 percent of most church problems come out of leadership. I didn't believe it then, but now I know it's true. Over the years I have sat and talked with hundreds of pastors about the problems in their churches. During our conversations they almost always mentioned some of their leaders' names—Deacon So-and-So, Elder So-and-So, Associate Pastor So-and-So, Choir Director So-and-So, Bus Captain So-and-So. Many of them then asked me, "Can you be too tough on your leaders?"

Do you know what I told them? "You can never be too tough on your leaders." Pastors need to be tougher on their leaders than they are on themselves because those leaders are with the sheep more than the pastors are. God refers to believers as *sheep* many times in His Word. (John 10:15; 21:17, among others.) When you become a leader in your church, you automatically become an example to the sheep. It's a package deal. You can't separate the two, even though some try.

A number of people want to be a leader, but some don't want

to be a godly example. For instance, when a certain guest preacher or prophet speaks at their church, these leaders want their front row seat *and* they want an extra seat so they can bring a friend. But when was the last time those leaders sat on the front row and brought a friend to church to hear the pastor?

Personally, I don't think a leader should sit beyond the second row in the church. One of the things I've learned about leading over the years is that when you lead, that means you're out in front. So how can you lead people when you sit behind them?

I've been taught there's a reason for everything, so a few years ago I began asking pastors about certain people I saw sitting in the back of the church while I was preaching. I noticed that they were not real interested in my message. In most cases I was told that the person sitting in the back was a leader in the church.

I figured they had to have a reason other than that they were designated to sit there. Most likely these leaders weren't sitting that far away from the pastor at first. Then I would meet with these pastors, and they would tell me they were having problems with the same leader who was sitting in the back. I believe the reason these leaders sit in the back is because they don't want the people to see that they don't get along with the pastor anymore.

Maybe the leaders disagree over some kind of change the pastor made. Perhaps they think the pastor should have waited at least three months before announcing it to the congregation. So they move to the back of the church to sit far away from the pastor because they're upset.

Here's one solution I suggest to pastors: pick a row in the sanctuary, and if the leaders ever sit somewhere beyond that row, have a meeting with them to discuss the situation because they're sending the pastor a message by their actions and creating a negative atmosphere in the services. There has to be reason they are putting distance between you and them.

BE FAITHFUL, COMMITTED, AND EXCITED

In many churches, when people first become born again, they're on fire for the Lord and eager to do almost anything the pastor asks of them. But as time goes on, it seems harder and harder to get some of them to serve God.

Let me give you an illustration. A person who has recently become born again comes to church and hears the pastor teach on faithfulness. This new Christian is all fired up about the message and thinks, *I want to be faithful. The pastor said that Proverbs 28:20 tells us the faithful shall abound with blessings. I sure want to abound with blessings. And I want to be more faithful than I am right now.* But this new Christian keeps running into some church leaders who don't want to be any more faithful than they are right now.

The next Sunday this new Christian comes to church and hears the pastor preach on being committed. Again this person is excited about the message, thinking, *I want to be committed to the Lord. I want to be sold out much more than I am right now.* But this person keeps running into those same leaders who don't want to be any more committed than they are now.

Then in the Wednesday evening service, the new Christian hears the pastor teach that we need to get excited about Jesus and reaching the world for Him, and this person thinks, *I want to be excited about that. I want to be more excited than I am right now!* But this new believer keeps running into the church leaders who don't want to be any more excited than they are right now.

Eventually, the new believer will think, *Forget it. Maybe there is something wrong with me for getting so excited about church and the pastor's messages. Maybe God dropped me on my head when I got saved. But I'd sure like to be a leader. Leaders get to do awesome things in the church like staying after the services, fellowshipping with the speakers, and going places with the pastor. In order to be a leader, maybe I just need to do what the leaders do in this church—so I'll just sit in the back of the auditorium and do nothing.*

This is the truth. For people in the church to grow in faithfulness and become more committed and more excited, the leaders have to become more faithful, more committed, and more excited than they are right now. As long as the leaders are moving forward, the people will move forward. As long as the leaders grow, the people will grow. But when leaders stop, the people stop.

When we hear our pastors put a demand upon the leaders in the church—perhaps expecting them to listen to a certain CD, read a particular book, attend a leadership meeting, or do any other church-related task the pastor asks them to do—we need to rejoice. Those demands will help them to grow and to move forward—and when they do, we will too.

GOD LOVES A CHEERFUL "PICKER UPPER"

I've often had pastors ask me, "Is it too much to expect church leaders to be tithers in the church?" I have a great answer for that question: "Do you want your members to be tithers? If your leaders are not tithers, I can guarantee you this—your church won't be tithers because people never go beyond their leadership."

If pastors find the offerings are down, they need to watch their ushers. Second Chronicles 9:4 says that the Queen of Sheba saw "his [Solomon's] ascent by which he went up into the house of the LORD." In other words, she saw his body language in church. It's a known fact that 85 percent of communication is done through the body. Next Sunday, check out the kind of bodily expressions your church leaders are displaying and you'll see this is true.

When the pastor stands on the platform and says, "It's offering time," how do ushers respond? As they come down the aisle do people think, *I don't want to put anything in the bucket. They look like they're at a funeral. They're probably going to take the offering out back and bury it somewhere!* If God loves a cheerful giver—and He does (2 Cor. 9:7)—then God loves a cheerful "picker upper."

While we're on the subject, why do some pastors have to train their ushers in every service? These pastors have to tell their ushers, sometimes two or three times, that it's offering time. They have to tell them to pass out the offering envelopes, to pass the buckets, and that if someone's hand is raised, it means the person wants an offering envelope—and most of these ushers have been taking offerings for months, maybe even years.

I believe the reason this happens is that these ushers are not givers themselves. Show me a tithing usher who believes that when you give, it'll be given back to you good measure, pressed down, shaken together, and running over (Luke 6:38), and I'll show you an usher who doesn't need to be told by the pastor in every service what to do when it's time to take the offering.

I don't know about you, but if I'm going to pay my tithes in church, I want the person who's going to pick it up to be a tither too. In fact, if the usher walks up to you first with the offering bucket and that bucket is empty, don't drop in your offering. Instead, hand that empty bucket right back because there should already be an offering envelope in there—the usher's.

SERVE WITH STYLE

The people who served in Solomon's house had a distinctive, impressive style. Does your ministry of helps impress visitors or drive them away?

APPAREL

The Queen of Sheba was so impressed with the servants' apparel that the Bible says she noticed what they were wearing—twice.

> **"When the queen of Sheba had seen...the attendance of his ministers, *and their apparel;* his cupbearers also, *and their apparel.*"**
>
> **2 Chronicles 9:4**

The *Message* Bible says that the ministers were "sharply dressed." Does that phrase come to mind when you see your church leaders? How about the way you dress if you are in church leadership? Even the cupbearers (the ones who put the water on the platform) were dressed sharply because the queen also noticed what they were wearing.

At this point you may be thinking, *Maybe somebody needs to tell her that God doesn't look at the outward appearance; He looks at the inward appearance.* (1 Sam. 16:7.) That may be true in most cases, but not for people in church leadership.

When you know you're coming into the house of God to serve

in the house of God, what is your attitude when you go to your clothes closet on a Sunday morning? Do you throw open the door, pick out any old wrinkled, mismatched, or casual-looking outfit, and think, *Oh well, at least it's clean.* That is a *careless* attitude. I'm sure you are glad that God doesn't have a careless attitude with you!

Surely you have something better in your clothes closet than just what's clean. I'm not saying we have to wear $500 suits or $700 dresses. Your best and my best might not be the same. Your best and my best might not cost the same amount of money. Maybe my clothes aren't made out of the fancy material your clothes are made out of. Wearing your best might be as simple as ironing your clothes. Some leaders would be amazed at what an iron could do to their shirts or blouses! I just think we ought to give God our best.

Since the Queen of Sheba brought up their apparel twice, I could mention something else here about dress. I've been to some churches where the leaders looked sloppy, and I thought, *They must have hired these leaders because they sure don't dress like the pastor and his wife.* If you're not sure how to dress to serve in church, follow the example of your pastor.

And a good point to remember is that dressing in the same style will bring out the theme of unity. When a visitor or congregation member sees that the pastor and the leadership are all dressed in the same excellent way, they will think, *This church really has their act together and is going places for God.*

WORSHIP TEAM AND MUSICIANS

These are the people who are responsible for leading us into the presence of God and are using music to prepare our hearts to receive the pastor's message. Yet I've been in some churches where I've seen them stand up on the platform for a half an hour or more, singing and playing songs about Jesus and about how wonderful God is, and they can't even smile.

I travel to speak in other churches all the time, and I admit that on several occasions I've felt like walking up to the musicians or the worship team when the service was over and asking, "Who are you mad at? What are you so upset about?"

Worship team members and musicians need to look as though they want to be up on the platform. Some of the excuses I've heard when I teach on this are, "You wouldn't believe what I'm going through," or "The reason I don't smile while I'm playing is because I'm concentrating on playing the music." Maybe they just need to practice more or spend time in prayer as a group before the services begin. But it is important that they show on the outside the joy of worshipping God on the inside. Otherwise, they won't inspire the congregation to worship God.

Worship team members should understand putting on a garment of praise for the spirit of heaviness (Isa. 61:3) more than anyone else. Whether they have practiced enough or not, whether they have had a bad week or not, they need to put their whole heart and soul into praising God. The people will never go where they don't lead them.

YOUTH PASTORS

You may be surprised to hear this, but our youth want good leaders too. I have a friend who's in ministry, and he called me to relate this story just after the church he attended had hired a new youth leader. One day, after his children had gone to the youth ministry meetings for a while, they came to my friend and said, "Dad, would you say something to our new youth leader?"

My friend said, "Why?"

"He cusses around us all the time," they replied. "He says the reason he does it is that he thinks it's cool. But Dad, it's not cool to us. Some of the kids have a reason if they cuss—they don't know any better. But he doesn't have a reason for doing it. He's supposed to show us the right way to live."

Have you ever been to a church where you can't tell the youth pastor from the youth? I have—many times. I'm not talking about when the youth-related activities and outreaches call for casual dress. I'm talking about those who always dress like teenagers. They also talk like them and walk like them. Then we wonder why our youth don't grow up.

I hear this from some youth pastors, "I'm just trying to get down to their level."

I tell them, "Well, you made it! The problem is, they don't have anybody to take them from that level to the next because you're trying to act like one of them."

Many youth pastors are doing a fantastic job in leading young people to grow emotionally and spiritually. But I believe that some youth pastors don't want to grow up. They don't want to have to take on responsibility as adults, and they've found a place where they can continue being a child.

Youth pastors should only get down on the kids' level when they are communicating the truth of God's Word. They need to say it in a way that their kids can understand it. At the same time, they need to challenge them to grow up and be godly adults—and they need to be an example of godly adults at all times. They can be "cool" and still be on fire for God.

This is not meant to be a condemning message, but I want to reveal areas in the church that might need improvement so you can change them. We're not going to win the world by offering them the same things they already have. We're going to win them by showing them there's something better.

STUDY NOTES

Leadership and Being a Godly Example

1. What is the "last club" we are all going to want to get into? How do you get into it?

2. If the leaders of a church are not faithful, will the rest of the congregation be faithful?

3. What are the only two acceptable excuses for a leader missing a service or meeting?

4. Where do most church problems come from?

5. Where should leaders sit and why?

Be Faithful, Committed, and Excited

6. Explain the process through which a new Christian can be influenced to either grow or backslide by the leaders in the church.

7. How important is it for the pastor to continually challenge the leaders of the church?

God Loves a Cheerful "Picker Upper"

8. What percentage of communication is body language?

9. How should ushers react outwardly when they take the offering?

10. Why is it important for ushers to understand giving?

Serve With Style

Apparel

11. What does the way you dress say to visitors and other members

of the church? Whose example should you follow?

12. What outward appearance can tell visitors and members of the church that your church has its act together?

Worship Team and Musicians

13. How does the outward appearance of the praise and worship team and musicians affect a congregation?

Youth Pastors

14. What can it mean when you cannot tell the youth pastor from the youth?

15. When is it appropriate for a youth pastor to come down to a kid's level, and when is it inappropriate?

12

STEPPING INTO
ANOTHER WORLD

Did you ever hear anybody say, "Well, I'm just going to have to see it to believe it"? That kind of logic led the Queen of Sheba on her long journey to Solomon's palace. After just one visit, she knew the truth and told Solomon, "It was a true report which I heard in mine own land of thine acts, and of thy wisdom" (2 Chron. 9:5). Sounds like someone talked to her, doesn't it? What she heard had drawn her to the house of God. Then what she saw when she got there changed her life.

> **Howbeit I believed not their words, until I came, and mine eyes had seen it: and, behold, the one half of the greatness of thy wisdom was not told me: for thou exceedest the fame that I heard.**
>
> **2 Chronicles 9:5**

There was something else that affected the queen just as much or more than what she had been seeing. Look what she said in the next verse.

Happy are thy men, and happy are these thy servants, which stand continually before thee, that hear thy wisdom.

2 Chronicles 9:7

Everywhere she went everybody was happy! The spirit of the place affected her. She couldn't get over their attitude. That said volumes about Solomon's leadership style and the conditions of the nation. The same holds true in our modern churches. A pastor can preach one of the most anointed messages he's ever preached, but it's the attitude of the ministry of helps that makes or breaks a church more so than the pastor.

"GOD'S IN THIS PLACE!"

Let's look at a church that knows all about the ministry of helps. The people who serve in that kind of church know that wherever they are, Jesus is there with them.

The greeters stand at the door with smiles on their faces, and the love of God is radiating from them to everyone they meet. A new family walks in, and the greeters shake their hands. They hug them. They answer all their questions and tell them where everything is located in the church. The family is touched, and as they walk away they say, "Wow, God's at the door."

That family walks on down the hall to the nursery. The nursery worker comes out with a big smile on her face, and she finds out they're new. "We just want to welcome you today to our church," she says. "Let me tell you some things about our nursery that you might not know."

"This is not a babysitting service back here; it's a ministry. What I mean is that we're going to be ministering the love of Jesus to your baby, as our pastor is going to be ministering the love of Jesus to you. We've got some information written up about our nursery that we'd like for you to read so you can see that we are well qualified to take care of your little one. We want you to have the peace of God because we believe that God brought you here, and we want to make sure you hear everything that God has to say to you today through our pastor."

As those parents walk away from the nursery, they're saying, "Wow, God's in the nursery!"

Now they come on down the hall to the children's church. The children's worker comes out with a smile on his face and finds out they're new. He says to them, "We just want to welcome you today to our church. Let me tell you some things about our children's ministry you might not know."

"We do more than just teach the children how many animals went into the ark," he says. "We also teach them the Word of God, as our pastor is going to teach you the Word of God today, and you're going to leave here a family full of the Word of God." The parents walk away going, "Wow, God's in children's church."

Finally, they walk into the sanctuary, and they see smiling ushers who are like the disciples who said to blind Bartimaeus, "Be of good cheer. The Master calls of thee" (Mark 10:49). They find this family a good seat up front and say to them, "You're new here and we want you to get up front so you can see and hear everything God has for you, because that's why God brought you to our church today. Our pastor's been in the Word and in prayer, and we're looking forward to another great 'meal' from him this Sunday morning." The ushers walk away and these parents go, "Wow, God's in the ushers."

Then the worship leader comes out. This person has already been with the sound person and had a sound check. The mic has already been turned up, so all the worship leader does is grab that mic and takes off singing.

This husband and wife are sitting there in wonder, and the wife begins to shake and the husband begins to shake, and they both look at each other and say, "What do you think is going to happen when the preacher comes out?" They've been so affected by the ministry of helps team that the pastor could pull out old Sermon Number Eight that doesn't have an ounce of anointing on it and that family would still keep coming back to that church!

Do you see it clearer now? *We're in this together.*

WHY ALL THE FUSS AND BOTHER?

At this point you may be saying, "I've been sitting here reading this book for a while now, and all I've heard is that we ought to dress right, act right, smell right, and look right. But why are we doing all of this? Are we just putting on a big show?" I'm glad you asked.

One phrase stood out to me when I read about the Queen of Sheba in 2 Chronicles 9:4: "There was no more spirit in her." Now, that doesn't mean she died. *The New American Standard Bible* version says, "She was breathless."

When she saw all the wonders of Solomon and his palace—the wisdom of Solomon, the house that he had built, the meat on his table, the sitting of his servants, the attendance of his ministers and their apparel, the cupbearers and their apparel, and the way he carried himself up into the house of the Lord—she was so astonished by it that it took her breath away. I wouldn't be surprised if she had the thought, *It's like stepping into another world.*

I've talked to countless people who have made that same positive comment to me about a certain church they visited. Isn't that what so many in the world out there are looking for—another world, one that is better?

You and I know there is a better world; it's called the kingdom of God. Why don't we, the church, show it to others? I know we could never fully show heaven to someone, but I personally believe that God gives every church one piece of the pie, and all we have to do is serve up *our* piece. If we can get the world to take a bite of the piece of our pie, they'll say, "You know, I want the whole pie."

God has given every believer the job of reconciling their world to Christ. (2 Cor. 5:18-20 NIV.) It's up to us to compel people to come to church (Luke 14:23)—and make sure that when they get there, they find out that there is a God and that His way of living is better. That's the message I've tried to share in this book. I think this next verse sums it up and captures the real purpose of the ministry of helps.

> **[The Queen of Sheba said,] Blessed be the LORD thy God.**
>
> **2 Chronicles 9:8**

Do you realize what this verse is saying? The Queen of Sheba got saved! I know nobody got born again in the Old Testament because Jesus hadn't yet come to earth, died on the cross for our sins, and rose again to sit at the right hand of God in heaven. But it's the type and shadow of what was to come in the New Testament; and those who believed were counted as saved, just like Abraham. (Rom. 4:3.) This first-time visitor only went to one "church," and she said, "There is a God."

I don't think an unsaved person should have to go to a church four or five times to realize that there is a God. They should realize it in their *first* visit. That's what church is all about. We're here to lift up Jesus and change our world by letting them know there is a better way to live—and it's in Him.

Look at what the Queen of Sheba realized from her visit with Solomon.

> God...delighted in thee to set thee on his throne, to be king for the LORD thy God: because thy God loved Israel, to establish them for ever, therefore made he thee king over them, to do judgment and justice.
>
> 2 Chronicles 9:8

What a statement from a first-time visitor! "There is a God. You're a man of God. This is a house of God. God's hand is upon you." But that wasn't all. After the altar call came the offering. This woman expressed the depth of her appreciation and admiration through her generous giving.

> And she gave the king an hundred and twenty talents of gold, and of spices great abundance, and precious stones: neither was there any such spice as the queen of Sheba gave king Solomon.
>
> 2 Chronicles 9:9

She pulled out her checkbook that morning, wrote a check for the equivalent of 130 million dollars, and dropped it in the bucket when it went by!

There's no telling how many Queens of Sheba have been to your church, people who could write just one check and pay for everything without even blinking an eye. Let me put it this way. If your church's buildings and land aren't paid for yet, I can tell you how to get them paid for. According to this Scripture, let the first-time visitors pay for it!

This happened to a pastor I know who had a large church in Texas. He was preaching one Sunday morning, and he gave an altar call to lay hands on people who were sick so he could pray for their healing. One of the people who came up for prayer was a visitor from California. When he came up to the altar, some of the leaders prayed for him without knowing that he was a visitor or where he was from. About six weeks later, the pastor received a call from this man. First, he told the pastor how blessed he had been at the church and how wonderful it was. Then he asked, "Pastor, is there anything you need in the church?"

It just so happened that the church was in a building program, so the pastor reluctantly said to this man who'd only been in the church once, "We do have a building program going on right now, and if you want to give a little to that, we would really appreciate it."

The man said yes, and in the mail about a week later the pastor received a check for $250,000 from him! But it didn't stop there. By the end of the year, the man had given almost one million dollars to that church—and he'd only stepped in the building one time!

Money is not the only point here. In fact, forget the money. Let's talk about people. The Queen of Sheba not only gave millions of dollars to Solomon, but some say that she was actually the one responsible for bringing the teachings of God to her country.

What am I saying? You don't know who's going to walk into your church service, and the impact that you make upon them may well determine the impact that they make upon other cities, other nations—and upon their world. The impact that you make upon them may just give them the boldness to go home and walk across the street and share Jesus with their neighbor.

I talked to a missionary couple one time who told me that it was in just one church service that God filled their hearts with love for the country they now serve. They said there would be times when they would be lying in a hut in that country, thinking, *I'm going to give up. I'm going to quit. This is just too difficult.* But then they would think about that *one* church service when God called them to the mission field, and they would say, "No, we won't quit. God, You're real! You're everlasting because Your love was everywhere in that church."

STUDY NOTES

Stepping into Another World

1. What was perhaps the most important thing that the Queen of Sheba saw when she visited Israel?

"God's in This Place!"

2. What does every minister of helps know?

3. How does God show His presence through every minister of helps?

Why All the Fuss and Bother?

4. Read 2 Chronicles 9:4. What happened to the Queen of Sheba as she experienced Solomon's court?

5. What is the main thing most visitors and unbelievers are looking for in a church?

6. Read 2 Chronicles 9:8. What was the first thing the Queen of Sheba did after she had seen Solomon's realm?

7. What is the purpose of putting our best foot forward outwardly as a church?

8. How did the Queen of Sheba show her appreciation for all that Solomon had shown her? How does this affect your thinking about the ministry of helps?

9. What did the Queen of Sheba take back to her country?

13

THE REWARDS
OF HELPING

Around 1985 Kathy and I went to Singapore to minister in a small church of 150 people, which was pastored by a young, single Singaporean. While we were there, I told him that if he ever came to the Tulsa area in the U.S. and needed a place to stay, he could stay with us. A few months went by, and he called to see if he could stay with us during a campmeeting in our city. Because I'm a man of my word, I said, "Sure."

We met him at the airport and put him in one of our daughters' bedrooms. Although he wasn't too keen on Barbie and Ken™, we had a wonderful time of fellowship and getting to know each other. On Sunday morning he came with me to open the church and get things ready for the services. During the week we took him to different ministries and churches in the area. Many of them blessed him with materials to take back to his church. We even took him to our friend's ranch, where he rode a horse for the first time in his life. He was quite a cowboy for the day.

In 2005 this same pastor flew me to Singapore (in business class) and put me in the Singapore Ritz Carlton hotel. Before I even preached, he gave our ministry an outstanding offering. By this time his church had about 13,000 members and was one of the greatest ministry of helps churches I had known. On Wednesday night we had a ministry of helps meeting. There were over 2000 in attendance and 800 were ushers! This great church even served a meal to their workers that evening.

Between two of the four Sunday morning services, the pastor looked at me and smiled. Then he said, "You never know who you will help."

A LESSON FROM THE RITZ

During my stay at the Ritz Carlton, I wanted to see with my own eyes why it is considered one of the best hotels in the world. I spent one to two hours a day sitting in the lobby watching how they treated their customers. The first thing that impressed me was that after arriving at 5 A.M., I was addressed by my name by at least five different employees. When I went to eat, I asked for a certain table, and the next day I was asked if I wanted that same table.

I learned later that each guest's preferences and needs

are recorded in a database. At the main door there are several employees—excuse me, ladies and gentlemen—waiting to assist customers when they enter the hotel. I was blessed to meet the manager of the ladies and gentlemen of the hotel. He told me that the reason they don't have signs in the hotel is because the staff takes customers to where they want to go in the hotel, answering all their questions.

They wanted to give each customer a personal touch. I got to meet many of the ladies and gentlemen and asked them how they liked working for the Ritz Carlton. Not one of them had anything negative to say. They all had hearts to serve and received joy from it. I was also shown a small card that had their creed on it. I thought how interesting it would be if this was practiced in the local church, so I wrote a Ministry of Helps Creed for churches.

MINISTRY OF HELPS CREED

1. (Name of church) is a place where the genuine care and comfort of our members and guests is our highest mission. We pledge to provide the finest personal service and facilities so that the people will fully enjoy the presence of the Lord and the teaching of His Word, that they may be in a position to receive everything they need from Him.

2. The members of (name of church) who are God's ministry of helps are vital to our service to God's children and those who

come to our church to be saved. By applying the principles of trust, honesty, respect, integrity, and commitment, we nurture and maximize their gifts and callings to the benefit of each individual and the entire body.

3. (Name of church) provides a ministry environment where diversity is valued, spiritual life in Jesus Christ is strengthened, individual callings are identified and fulfilled, and all the glory and honor goes to God.

4. A minister of helps will warmly greet each member and visitor, using their name when possible. If they cannot answer their questions or meet their needs, they will direct them to the person or persons who can. When people exit our church, ministers of helps will warmly say good-bye, using their names if possible. Every person is treated with the utmost care and respect.

5. Every minister of helps will be trained by an experienced minister of helps. Leaders in the ministry of helps will always be open to the suggestions of others. If a minister of helps discovers an area that needs improvement or has a problem, they should report it to the appropriate leader. An attitude of humility and teamwork is essential to all ministers of helps.

6. Every minister of helps is an ambassador of (name of church) to their world outside of the church, just as they are an ambassador for Christ in the world. Helps ministers are to be as loyal to the church and their leadership in the church as they are to

the Lord Jesus Christ.

7. Ministers of helps pay particular attention to appearance in all things: dress, manner, and communication. They conform their dress and grooming to that of their leadership, which portrays unity. Their manners always consider the feelings and needs of others before themselves. Their communication is always polite, positive, and warm.

8. All ministers of helps must know and adhere to the safety standards of (name of church). This not only means creating and maintaining a safe environment for all members and visitors of the church, but also knowing all fire, security, and emergency procedures. They must know what to do in any problem situation.

9. Each minister of helps must take pride in (name of church) by conserving energy, properly maintaining all facilities, and generally protecting the property and environment.

10. Every minister of helps must understand their vital importance as a member of (name of church) and as a member of the universal body of Christ. Without them, Jesus cannot move through His body effectively, bring in His harvest of souls, and establish His kingdom in the earth.

In my travels to over 2500 churches, I've noticed the ones with the biggest hearts to serve others were doing the most in the kingdom of God. Hebrews 13:2 says that we could be entertaining angels without knowing it when we serve people. Serving others is what Jesus did while He was here on earth, and He did it without expecting anything in return. We must have that same attitude in serving. Then we will see even greater success than the Ritz Carlton because we are doing all things for the Lord.

BE WHAT GOD WANTS YOU TO BE

How do we get God to move through us as believers to impact others in a powerful, life-changing way? It's really very simple, and it's the very heart of this message.

Be what God wants you to be. If God has asked you to be in the ministry of helps—if He's asked you to be a nursery worker or an usher or a musician or the church cleaner or the church van driver or a servant in some other area—be the best you can be!

And then be happy in doing it. Take joy in fulfilling God's will for your life because He takes joy in watching you fulfill His will.

Do these things, and God will take care of the rest—the salvation of souls, the deliverance of those in bondage, the healing of bodies, the miracles, signs, and wonders, and everything else that displays His kingdom of love to a lost and dying world.

Be what God wants you to be. Do all that God wants you to do. Then nobody will be mad but the devil!

I can't think of a better way to conclude this chapter than to repeat this wonderful quote from Godbey:

Oh! The infinite value of the humble gospel helpers. Thousands of people who have no gifts as leaders are number-one helpers. How grand revival work moves along when red-hot platoons of fire-baptized helpers crowd around God's heroic leaders of the embattled hosts.

STUDY NOTES

The Rewards of Helping

1. Give an example from your life (or someone else's life) where you (they) helped or ministered to someone in need, and your (their) efforts brought great reward.

A Lesson From the Ritz

2. What is the first thing that impressed the author when he stayed at the Ritz Carlton hotel?

3. Name several other things that impressed him.

4. What does the Ritz Carlton hotel call their employees?

5. Would you like to stay at the Ritz Carlton hotel? Why?

Be What God Wants You to Be

6. What two things can every believer do to impact others in a powerful, life-changing way?

14

GENERAL PRINCIPALS
AND GUIDELINES

In every seminar I teach, there are generally some questions about principles and guidelines on choosing helpers and dealing with them. Following are some of the general guidelines I usually give pastors and church leaders.

Simply accepting everyone who wants to be an usher or door greeter is as dangerous as accepting someone who offers to sing in the choir — then finding out the person cannot carry a tune.

The atmosphere in your church will benefit from heading off possible areas of strife and confrontation before they happen. So, how do you know which people really are called to a ministry of helps and, if so, where to put them?

At one church where I was involved, my job was to find a place for people who wanted to help. The first thing I did was try to find out their true motives and attitudes.

I had a plaque on my wall that read, *Be leery of those who seek authority, but grab hold of those who want responsibility.*

So the first question I asked any volunteer was, "We are cleaning the church next Saturday. Can you be here for that?"

Some people only wanted to be teachers. They wanted authority. Another way of finding out people's motives was, for example, if they offered to usher, letting them read the guidelines for ushers. Sometimes that made them certain they wanted to usher; other times, it let them realize beforehand that they did not want to.

After you set someone into a position, the only way out—if he or she does not work out—usually is strife. And strife may take them out of the church as well as out of the position. If they know in advance what is expected, it helps to weed out those who are not sincere.

Also, the church leadership needs to place value on what the helps ministries are doing. People will do what the church leadership does. If your pastor is not respected in the church, it is because the leadership does not respect him or her. Leaders are an example. If there is strife in the church, you can pretty much tell there is strife in the leadership.

Another bottom line is: When a person is anointed, he or she brings forth fruit, and the fruit will define the office or duty in the church. The fruit of the life will label the person. People bearing fruit will not need a pastor to label them.

Pastors, you must present the whole vision of the church and ministry to the people. And you must trust your workers. If you seek the Lord concerning His will for placing anyone in a position, and if you find out the motives and attitudes of those who offer to work, it will be a peaceful situation. You will not place people where they are not supposed to be or where they will not work.

I would strongly suggest writing out guidelines for each position; then people know what is expected of them and what is not. Otherwise, how will your workers know what you want them to do?

Knowledge eliminates fear. If anyone has fear, it is usually because of the unknown. Giving your people knowledge will eliminate many fears of "What if? What if?" Training, also, is really important. We took two years to train workers in one church where I was involved.

But remember, *Jesus is a shepherd, not a dictator.* Therefore, He will rule—and you should rule—out of the level of submission to you, *not by force.* The more you submit to Him, the more He will use you. But Jesus will not *force* you to serve Him. And you cannot *force* workers to serve. Be consistent and firm with your helpers and associates, but do not be overbearing. That is how to build trust. If they do not trust you, they will not be able to feel confident in what they are doing.

ANSWERING THE CALL

Some of you may be thinking, *When I am equipped, I'll do what God wants me to do. I'm not ready now.*

> **For God hath not given us the spirit of fear; but of power, and of love, and of a sound mind.**
>
> **2 Timothy 1:7**

These three things are the usual excuses pastors hear from people not wanting to move out in their callings: I don't have the ability. I can't do it in love. Or I'll go crazy (if it is dealing with children)!

However, if God is calling you to do something, and you step out in faith, He will honor your obedience by giving you the love, ability, and lack of fear to do it. At first, you may be shaky and uncertain, but soon, it will seem as if you have always done this job. You will look back and wonder how you could have been fearful about it.

First of all, everyone in the helps ministry needs a close relationship with Jesus. You are in the church to serve God, and through His will, place, and timing, to serve your brothers and sisters in the Lord. But you are not there to please men.

Secondly, you need to keep looking at your ministry with a fresh eye. When I worked in a church at anything, about every three months, I would stop and look at what I was doing and why.

I would ask myself these questions: "Who put me here? Did I put myself here or did God?"

There have been many times when I would have to swallow hard and admit it was me; then I would go to those in charge and ask to be taken out of that position. That is not easy to do. The best way is to be sure ahead of time that God is placing you there.

Placing yourself in an area is where the turmoil starts and trouble begins. Sooner or later, you will leave that position, or be asked to, and that is usually where strife enters. If you are in the wrong area, admit you have made a mistake and peacefully move out. If where you are is a mistake, it was your idea. God does not make mistakes.

Once, as an usher, I had the responsibility of putting water on the platform. At one point, I felt I had grown beyond putting water on the platform, so I gave that job to another usher. Later, when I took a look at myself, I had to ask who had prompted me to give up the water detail—me or God? I had to admit it was me. So I had to go back to the other usher, apologize, and ask if I could again put water on the platform until I was relieved of that by the Holy Spirit or the head usher.

To maintain your spiritual walk, it is vital that you stop

periodically and check yourself.

Did God put you where you are, or did you put yourself there?

Did God tell you to leave the place where you are, or did the flesh just get bored and want to do something new?

15

QUESTIONS AND ANSWERS ON THE MINISTRY OF HELPS

One question that I hear frequently is: How do you distinguish between a call to a certain ministry and seeing a need that you have the ability to meet? Another frequent question is: How do you know what to do when you have the ability and are available to do a job, but you already are involved in something else?

In either case, my advice is to just pick up the phone and volunteer to do whatever is needed. People use the phrase, "Well, I'm just not called in that area" to avoid helping out. You were called the day you got saved. When you were born again, you were adopted through the Lord Jesus Christ into the family of God. His family is no different than an earthly family in this respect: If the whole family prospers and loves one another, then every family member has to pitch in and help.

Suppose your mother said to you as a child, "I need the beds made and the dishes washed," or your dad said, "I need the garbage carried out," or whatever.

Would you have told them, "I'm sorry, but I've not been called in that area"?

Of course not. Then why do we think we can put off our heavenly Father that way when He has chores that need doing?

I have never been "called" to this ministry. I just began to do the things God told me to do. I did not want to do all of them, but I do what He brings me to do. God does not move on behalf of status; He moves on behalf of His servants.

So many people want a "calling." As a Christian, you want to serve God. That is a calling in itself. If you move out and "do what your hand finds to do" (1 Samuel 10:7), God will begin to speak to your heart about the area where He wants to use you. A car has to be in gear and moving before you can turn it in a certain direction.

When I took a position on the staff of a large church some years back after having been in a traveling ministry for several years, some people told me I was moving backward. I was concerned about that, and one day as I was flying somewhere, I asked the Lord if I was moving backward.

He said, "Buddy, how much money are you budgeting for the six departments that you oversee right now?"

I said, "A million and a half dollars."

He said, "When was the last time you had to handle $1.5 million?"

I said, "Lord, I guess I'm moving forward, not backward!"

DOOR GREETERS

Q. As a greeter, is it inappropriate to say, "Good morning, how are you?" I feel as if I am putting people on the spot. What is a better way to greet people?

A. What you are saying sounds fine to me. Jesus answered a lot of questions with questions. If you are too "gushy" or sound phony, nothing you say will give them a genuine sense of welcome. Just be real, and greet people the way you would like to be greeted.

Q. How would you handle dress codes for greeters and ushers? And, when you set codes, what about those who think you are getting legalistic? Is there a good way to get your point across without sounding like, "If you don't like it, leave"?

A. One thing to begin with: If you are going to write guidelines, follow them, because once you compromise, you might as well throw them away. Some Christians who are young in the Lord will try to see how far they can go. In that case, you will just have to tell them, in love, that this is the way it is in your church. But communicate with them.

I am a firm believer that each department should have its own guidelines because each department has different needs. If you make one dress code and guideline for the whole church, you have eliminated a lot of people from participating. For example, in the nursery, the babies and toddlers could care less if you have on a suit and tie, or a dress and hose. They just care if your hands are warm and your voice loving.

Years ago, I was pretty adamant about ushers wearing suits and ties. Then I was preaching in a church in Spokane, Washington, and a man from Idaho came up to me after the service.

He said, "Brother Bell, I understand what you are saying about ushers and dress, but I don't really think there is a tie in the whole town I come from."

I went home and prayed, and the Holy Spirit spoke this to me: "Use the pastor and his wife as a dress code example. What they wear is what the ushers or greeters should wear, because they are before the people also."

Once a man came to me and so sincerely wanted to be an usher, but he did not have a suit or tie. In this church, there were thirty-five ushers. If I had bent the rules for this one man, the next week, I would have had them all in my office wanting to know why they had to wear ties, yet he did not.

So I said, "Why don't we find you a job in the church where you don't need a suit and tie, and we'll believe God for a suit and tie for you," and he agreed.

About two months later, one day after service, he came

running up to me with something in his hand and said, "Brother Bell, someone gave me a suit and tie today. Can I be an usher now?" He was one of the best ushers we ever had there.

When I did not bend the rules and let him usher according to his circumstances, that put value on being an usher. Often, we as pastors and leaders do not put value on working in the church. We treat it as a *have-to*, not a privilege.

NURSERY WORKERS

Q. Suppose all your life you have wondered what you are supposed to be doing. Then you get saved, and you are five years into your Christian walk, but you still do not know. However, all your life you have had this idea in the back of your mind that you want to work in the nursery. Yet you are not sure you like children or that you can communicate with them. Do you still wait to try your hand at the church nursery, feeling you are not yet ready? Or do you do it now, trusting God?

A. What is happening in your case is what we talked about earlier, fear: "I do not have the ability," and "I'll go crazy." Move out, and trust God to help you!

Q. What if you do not have enough nursery workers to maintain a one worker for every six children ratio?

A. Well, obviously, you must do with what you have. Pray for more helpers. And I would take only as many babies as you can effectively minister to and care for.

187

Q. Do you recommend that children's workers do extra activities outside the church? And do you recommend taking—say, forty children—outside all at once?

A. That is a question for your pastor to decide. However, if I were a pastor, I would look at the limitations of the church and the transportation. Also, the pastor must consider the responsibility involved and whether such practical things as insurance are in order.

When I worked in one large church, they had eight buses when I began to oversee the helps ministries—and only two of them ran. I proposed to clean them up. I called a bus company and had them pick up four of the buses and all of the other junky vehicles people had given the church. We began to believe God for good buses. When I left that church, there were five top-of-the-line buses that ran, and they were on a monthly maintenance program.

When a Christian school team went on an activity, they went on the number-one bus, and that did something for those kids. The buses were washed and cleaned out every week. The drivers were required to pass the city bus driver's test. So what you do with the children depends a lot on the equipment and trained personnel that you have.

Q. How can I get nursery workers together to pray before the service, and how can I meet with them without the distraction of the children?

A. Have your people come in a few minutes early and arrange for someone else to look after the children of the nursery workers for the few minutes you need. Or, you might rotate your workers, having one watch the children each service while the others meet. Have the workers purpose to pray on the way to church.

Q. I know nursery workers are important in the natural, but are they important in the spiritual area?

A. I saw a mother get saved one time as a result of the nursery worker. The worker did not lead her to the Lord, but the mother had attended church and left her baby in the nursery. All that week, the baby had been so good that the next Sunday that mother asked the nursery worker what on earth she had done to the baby. The nursery worker told her it was just Jesus in her baby and His love that had been felt by the baby. The woman went into the service and got saved. So, if you have a responsibility, take care of it. Do not neglect it because it does not seem important. You may get to heaven before you find out all of the results of your faithful obedience in the nursery—or in other areas.

Q. You stress the importance of having good people work in the nursery, but some churches use teenage girls. Do you think that is a good idea?

A. Usually, it is not hard to get teenage girls to work in the nursery. Do you know why? Because they are on the threshold of adulthood and they may not be comfortable in the adult services. The pastor and the Word of God are pushing them to step through to adulthood, and it is easier to stay on the child side. So to do that, they will volunteer to work in the nursery without realizing why. If you do not have quality children's workers, begin to pray for God to send you some.

Q. Is it not important for the workers to also hear the messages? If a helps ministry, such as nursery or ushers, works every service, when do they get to hear the Word of God?

A. That is a very good point. If your workers do not get the Word of God in them to build faith, their works will die. Do not work them until they die spiritually. Do not work people until they do not come back to church, and then shrug it off as their problem. The problem was they had someone over them who did not care about them. First Corinthians 12:25 says:

> That there should be no schism in the body; but that the members should have the same care one for another.

Have your workers rotate: work one service and attend the next. I know that takes a lot of workers, but that is an ideal to work toward.

PARKING

Q. How do you keep people from parking in spaces marked reserved for the handicapped?

A. Well, usually you feel like flattening their tires! But, of course, you cannot do that, not legally nor in Christian love. The key again is communication. However, it is amazing how many people drive onto church property and think the laws of the land no longer apply.

In an instance like this, I would just be standing near the car when that person came out of church. Then I would explain that by parking there, they may have kept some handicapped person from hearing a word from God that he or she needed that very day. If they do it again, you meet them again after the service. It will not take but a time or two until they will begin to find another space.

Just remember not to lose your cool. Many times these situations are real tests of the fruit of the Spirit within you. Also, if you do not get rude or mean with the people, they cannot complain to the pastor about you.

PRAISE AND WORSHIP LEADERS

Q. Are your singers and praise and worship leaders also in the helps ministry? And how should they operate with the pastor and with visiting speakers?

A. Yes, even the musicians are in the helps ministry. Hopefully, they set themselves to work under the pastor, not to do their own thing. The music and the rest of the service should flow together. This is a team operation, not a group of individuals following their own paths.

Concerning visiting speakers: the praise and worship leader should be willing to ask if the songs he or she has picked fit with the message. And it would be helpful if the pastor would find out from his guest how he (or she) likes the music to be, or how he (or she) feels the music should be during this service. Most ministers would really appreciate this.

I have had music people put the congregation to sleep, and it might take me thirty minutes into my message or teaching to get them spiritually awake. Perhaps if the musicians had come to me, we could have worked together to quickly get the people "up" in the spirit and ready to receive from the Lord.

Some churches where I have spoken, I have "come out running," then after a few minutes, looked back, and they were all still at the starting gate. Then I had to backpedal and pick them up.

I have been in services where only the last song wakes people up. There is nothing wrong with a worship service, if that is the way the Holy Spirit is moving. My point is: do not work against the speaker, whether he is quiet or excitable. A very helpful thing for pastors to do is ask the visiting speaker to pray for the workers before the service. That brings a unity between them.

USHERS

Q. One thing I find difficult is that often, when I ask people if I can take them to a seat, they say no. Then I watch them look all over the church and perhaps take five or more minutes to find a seat. What would be a good way to handle that situation?

A. A lot of times, roping off sections and opening them only as needed will solve that. Or, you could have an usher stand at a row until it is filled, then move to the next one. Some people just do not like to be escorted, and you will have some sheep jump the gate. Just do not lose your salvation over it! Ushers really have to be on their toes because they handle the public.

People who attend may not all be members. Some may not even be Christians. As an usher, your attitude should be kind and peaceable. If you are easily offended, you need to let God deal with that before you move into any kind of public position.

People who come to church have been at work all week, perhaps being yelled at by bosses, so that they are already touchy. Realize that, and be prepared. Everyone you seat, or try to seat, is not going to be an angel. Your job is to minister to them through your attitude so they will be able to receive the Word of God.

Q. I would like to know how you handle chronic problems. For example, how do you handle people who sit in the roped-off areas or hold up the back wall? How do you deal with people who continually walk out of the service and spend a lot of time outside the auditorium against the obvious wishes of the congregation and the pastor?

A. I am a great believer in communication. I discovered through trial and error that if you will go and talk to that person, there may be a reason for getting up and leaving. Perhaps it is medical. If so, try to arrange to give them a particular seat on the aisle in order that their moving in and out will not distract others. And explain to them about distraction. Tell them nicely and lovingly that one little distraction might cause someone to miss the one Word from God that He brought them there to receive that day. As far as those who sit in roped-off areas, you only have two alternatives: leave them alone or ask them nicely to move.

Q. You told once of an incident when you were assaulted while you were speaking. What could a good usher have done to keep that situation from getting as far as it did?

A. The ushers did not move quickly enough in this instance. Also, there were two women ushers at each side of where this happened, and they were really upset. I do not believe women ushers should be by themselves. Pair them with a man, instead, simply because of possibilities like this.

The minute this man got up and began to talk or move, if I had been working as an usher, I would have approached him and placed my hand upon his shoulder. Instead, the ushers held back, giving the man time to get to me and begin to hit and bite me—and even then, there was no one there to help. He should have been stopped and removed.

You may have, or be in, a small church right now, but your

church will grow, and you will not know everyone. That is when the devil will begin to slip in troublemakers or begin to stir up demonic disturbances. They could be worse than simply creating a scene.

Pastors have been shot in services. One evangelist tells of a man coming into one of his services with a pistol, planning to shoot him. But in prayer beforehand, the Lord revealed this to the ushers. So they were able to recognize the man and remove him. One pastor told me his first experience like this was as a teenager when an ex-con came into church looking for his wife. He shot the pastor with a double-barreled shotgun, then found his wife and shot her. The pastor said no one moved to try to stop the guy. The congregation just sat there in shock and let it happen.

As an usher, if you get a check in your spirit about someone, keep an eye on him. Do not kick him out without obvious reason, but be sure he sits where you want him to sit—right beside an usher.

MISCELLANEOUS SUBJECTS

Q. When you have an altar call, and 150 people come forward, how can you organize things without quenching the Holy Spirit?

A. The organization should come before the people come forward. Do not wait until you already have them standing around the altar before you figure out how to handle the ministry.

Meet with your ushers and counselors, and arrange who is to be where and what each is to do before you have meetings where large numbers may end up at the altar or up front to be ministered to.

In addition, if you have a visiting speaker in your church, tell him or her ahead of time what room to send people to if there is an altar call. Visiting speakers will not know whether your ushers or counselors are prepared. If it looks as if there is no planned organization, they may hold back and that will quench the Spirit of God.

It is a good idea to write down on a file card your preparations for contingencies that might arise in a meeting and give it to a visiting speaker. Make a note of such things so your praise and worship leader or pianist is attuned to the Spirit and can flow with His moves, as well as whether you have another room to send people, and whether you have trained counselors.

Q. Does helps go beyond working in the church?

A. Yes, rendering assistance or giving help to the weak or the needy also qualifies. I even believe anyone who is doing their day-to-day work is operating in the ministry of helps. God will help you on your job. You are a Christian at work as well as in church and at home. Some people try to fit church into their lives: "If I have time, I'll go to church." I do not think that way. Everything I do is centered around God and His work. Before

I was in full-time ministry, I expected God to help me on my job.

I already was operating in the ministry of helps when I learned about it. The helps ministry goes beyond the four walls of the sanctuary. When you are prompted to render assistance or give help to the sick or needy, that is God working. A lot of people are moved by the Holy Spirit to do such things, but then they take the credit themselves.

Q. What about the ministry of governments?

A. I believe the ministry of governments has not been fully tapped yet. Governments and helps are to work and flow together. Governments deals with leadership and should be emphasized in today's church just as much as helps.

Q. How do you deal with a supervisor who is trying to put onto you things that are his job or things he does not want to do?

A. About the only thing you can do is pray for hidden things to be brought to light (1 Cor. 4:5), pray for God to bring what is happening to the attention of someone in leadership. In the meantime, keep your attitude consistent with the fruit of the Spirit, and do the work as best you can.

If you become a supervisor, be certain to keep your attitude right. Sometimes we think we know better how to direct someone else's life than that person does. We need to pay attention to our shortcomings, not others' shortcomings: Am I where God wants me? Am I doing what God wants me to do?

I used to think, Okay, *God, You can sit down. I'll take care of this.*

Then I found out that He wants to be involved in the church. He wants to handle things. Just take care of yourself, and God will take care of your brother.

I was teaching along this line one day, and a woman came up to me and said, "Brother Bell, I'm kind of upset with you."

I said, "Oh, no! I thought everyone loved me."

She said, "See those two people sitting together back there? I have been working with them for months, and because of your little teaching today, I'm going to have to start all over again!"

I said, "Well, Ma'am, I'm sorry I interfered with your guinea pigs."

And that is exactly what those two people were to her. She was running their lives. It is time we let God back into the church. It is time we let people hear from God. Clay cannot shape clay. Only the Potter shapes and molds us.

Q. How do you get people in the church to work?

A. Sometimes the only thing that motivates people is examples. Some people are working in churches today because of seeing me and my wife work and be committed.

Q. If they have an example, how do you keep them from copying the example? How do you get them to follow their own paths?

A. Pastors in general need to learn how to manage people. I can go into a lot of churches and motivate people to get behind the pastor. However, what happens when I leave many times is that the pastor does not know what to do with them.

I am not talking about manipulating people. I am talking about *leading* them, getting them into the Word of God, *expecting* them to do certain things. That is what motivates people.

Leaders should be saying, "I want you to be a success. I want you to fulfill everything God has for you," not, "You're *going* to be a success; do you hear me?"

Give people a positive goal to reach toward, not a negative one. For many years, leaders have presented the negative. You cannot fight the negative with the negative. You have to overcome evil with good. Teach them something positive. Fight the negative factor in their lives with the positive.

This subject came up in a pastor's conference in Florida early in the 1980s, and the Lord spoke forth in a prophecy:

There are those of you here, saith the Lord, who wonder how to inspire in your workers the loyalty and dedication you have seen demonstrated here. Here is the key. If you will submit yourself to Me, and discipline yourself to follow Me closely, showing unto Me the same loyalty and commitment you desire your workers to show toward you, then I, the Lord, will inspire your workers to show that same loyalty and submission to you.

To the same extent that you submit yourself to Me, I will inspire them to submit to you. Do not try to force them or manipulate them into being submissive. If you will simply set your eyes on Me and follow Me closely, then without any conscious effort on your part, I, the Lord, will move upon men's hearts to follow you as you follow Me and serve you as you serve Me. It is that simple, saith the Lord.

16

COMMENTS FROM
MINISTRY OF HELPS SEMINARS

• I am just seeing how disorganized I have been. I am the leader of the ministry of helps, which I did not realize until I came to this meeting. I am excited, and I am believing for the zeal of God to return to my life so I can impart it to those who are under me. I want to see the ministry of helps really come forth in our church.

• I, too, have been serving in helps and did not know it until now. I have come so alive and on fire to share this with everyone else in our church. I see them doing the same thing—serving but not knowing that is what God has called them to do.

• I feel like a sponge, absorbing all of this revelation. I am so blessed that the Lord sent me here in order for me to take this back to my church. The main thing I want to share with them is that they are not just workers. This is a ministry. They are not just cleaning the church. The Lord knows what they are doing. The Lord sees their hearts.

• Sunday morning before I came to this seminar, I was in the front of the auditorium patching some cords for the sound system, and I was really "burning" inside. The pastor asked me what was wrong.

I said, "It just seems as if the people in the ministry of helps aren't doing their part."

He said, "Well, it comes off sounding as if you are mad at me or something."

Now, I see that I was not even doing my job. So I am motivated to do my job right and be an example.

• One thing I have learned is that we all go through the same things. I had never known what I was supposed to do in the ministry, like many others here. I spent three years asking God what He wanted me to do. I did not know that stepping into helping is a ministry.

People miss God so badly sometimes. They look way out there at the horizon, and the ministry is right at their feet. They do not know they are already in the will of God passing the bucket, changing diapers, or cleaning the church. You are in the will of God if you put all you have into what you are doing.

Early in my Christian life, I received a prophecy that said I would go around the world spreading the Word of God. Now, I have learned that I can be just where God wants me in the ministry by doing what I can right where I am. When I do what He tells me to do, then He will promote me according to what He wants.

• I have learned that encouragement and motivation come from the inside, not the outside. I had gotten stale, and I now realize it was not on account of my surroundings. I can rely on God to motivate me and to encourage me.

The other thing that I can take back with me is that helps is not just one department, one area of the church. Helps is being willing to do whatever is needed at any time.

17

INTRODUCTION:
HOW TO USE THE
STUDY COURSE

The Ministry of Helps Study Course is designed to help the believer understand in greater depth the truths brought forth in the Word of God concerning the ministry of helps.

This program of study is based on outlines that I use in teaching a three-day seminar on this subject.

The study course in this book includes three weeks of study materials with five lessons a week, one for each day. To gain the most from this study, you should complete only one lesson each day.

After each lesson, you will find several questions. Answer each one carefully, taking time to think before you answer. The questions are designed to teach you how to meditate on God's Word.

You meditate on a teaching by carefully considering each important point of the lesson. Make sure you understand in your heart what the Holy Spirit has brought to you specifically.

According to David, king and psalmist, those who meditate on God's Word day and night are the ones who will prosper in this life.

> But his delight is in the law of the Lord; and in his law doth he meditate day and night.
>
> And he shall be like a tree planted by the rivers of water, that bringeth forth his fruit in his season; his leaf also shall not wither; and whatsoever he doeth shall prosper.
>
> Psalm 1:2,3

The Hebrew word *hagah* translated in this psalm as *meditate* means "to murmur, to mutter ... to meditate, to muse, to speak, to praise; to whisper."[1] The biblical *meditate* obviously does not have the meaning common usage gives it today: that of sitting quietly, or in some cases, even going into a trance-like state of mind.

To be certain you have all of the illumination or revelation the Holy Spirit wants you to have out of these lessons, praise the Lord after you study, and thank Him for His Word. Then read the lessons out loud and consider them. Find any scriptures that come to your mind, or are given along with the lesson, and mentally

---

[1] Sodhiates, *The Greek-Hebrew Key Study Bible* (Grand Rapids: Baker Book House, AMG Publishers, 1984), p. 1587. 8

chew them over as a cow chews her cud.

If you will take these lessons seriously and with a teachable spirit, this course will help you prosper in the ministry of helps.

18

WEEK ONE:
WHAT IS THE
MINISTRY OF HELPS?

DAY ONE: DEFINING THE MINISTRY OF HELPS

And God hath set some in the church, first apostles, secondarily prophets, thirdly teachers, after that miracles, then gifts of healings, helps, governments, diversities of tongues.

1 Corinthians 12:28

The ministries that we call "the five ministry gifts," are to help the church grow. However, all of the jobs designated by the Lord must be done if God's goal for His family is to be reached.

If you are born again, you are part of God's family. As part of the family of God, have you ever wondered what your place might be in the family? Or have you ever wanted to be able to help your brothers and sisters in the Lord?

Do you have a desire to be part of God's mighty move in these last days?

God indeed has called you to a very important ministry—the ministry of helps. Notice in 1 Corinthians 12:28 what the Holy Spirit spoke through the apostle Paul about the helps ministry:

1. It is a supernatural ministry, listed among things such as miracles and healings.

2. It is a "gift" God has set in the church like a concrete pillar to hold things up.

Who Do You Help?

You may be wondering, If I am in the helps ministry, who do I help?

You help the one God has set in each church to oversee it. Your job is to help your pastor run the church. Helps ministries act like fingers on a hand in assisting pastors.

The Lord has given your pastor a vision for his church, and He has given you to your pastor to "help" bring that vision to pass. Without the helps ministry, things will not get done. A pastor without those set to help him would be like a hand without fingers.

DAY ONE STUDY QUESTIONS

1. What kind of list is given in 1 Corinthians 12:28?

2. Who set helps in the church?

3. What was God's purpose in setting helps ministries in the

church?

4. Who does the helps ministry help?

5. What can happen to a church with no helps ministry?

DAY TWO: THE PURPOSE OF THE HELPS MINISTRY

And he gave some, apostles; and some, prophets; and some, evangelists; and some, pastors and teachers;

For the perfecting of the saints, for the work of the ministry, for the edifying of the body of Christ.

Ephesians 4:11,12

Have you ever wondered why God set apostles, prophets, evangelists, pastors, and teachers in the church?

Paul made it clear in his letter to the church at Ephesus that the ministry gifts were put in the body of Christ for one main purpose: to perfect (or mature) the saints.

People who are maturing, growing up in Christ, will exhibit two qualities:

1. They will build up and add to the welfare of God's family, the church.

2. They will learn to minister—to help or serve—others.

You can tell the truly mature Christians in every situation by those who help the pastor, not hinder him. Given the opportunity through your prayers and support, God will enable your pastor or pastors to equip and perfect you with everything you need to function supernaturally in the ministry of helps.

DAY TWO STUDY QUESTIONS

1. What are the five ministry gifts in Ephesians 4:11?
2. How many of these are gifts from God to the church?
3. What is the main purpose of these ministries in the church?
4. What is another word for *perfecting*?
5. What are the two qualities of those maturing in Christ?
6. How can you tell who the truly mature Christians are in the church?
7. Who does God use to equip and perfect you for works of service to His church?
8. Why did God give you a pastor in your church?

DAY THREE: ONE WHO GIVES ASSISTANCE

God Himself set the ministry of helps in the body of Christ, as we saw from 1 Corinthians 12:28. Helps is a supernatural ministry with its own supernatural anointing to serve God by serving His pastors and His people.

The definition of helps literally is "one who gives assistance."

If someone in your church needs help, and you can meet that need, do it! That will keep your pastor from having to do it.

Satan delights in keeping a pastor so busy that he cannot lead the people as he ought to do. Your obedience to God's call for the helps ministry will protect your pastor from this dangerous snare. God wants to speak to His people through the pastor, but He cannot if the pastor is too busy to spend time in prayer.

In Numbers 11:10-17, we read how God set the ministry of helps into His people of that day—Israel. Moses could no longer help the people individually. There were too many of them with too many problems.

Moses cried out to God about the burden of all these people upon him (v. 11), and God answered. The Lord told Moses to pick seventy elders of the people and bring them before Him. Then the Lord said He would take off the spirit which is upon thee, and will put it upon them (v. 17) in order that the elders might share the burden of the people.

The seventy elders were given a supernatural ability to share the load of caring for God's people. Doing the things that will benefit the pastor takes a supernatural anointing. Ask God for this anointing, and He will gladly answer. God's vision is the one He gave your pastor, so help the pastor fulfill that to the glory of the Lord.

DAY THREE STUDY QUESTIONS

1. What is the definition of the ministry of helps?
2. What benefit does your pastor receive when you help others

in the church?

3. What does Satan delight in doing to pastors?

4. Why did Moses cry out to God (Num. 11:10-17)?

5. How did God answer him?

6. What did the Lord give the seventy elders of Israel whom Moses chose to help him?

7. In Numbers 11:17, what did God say to Moses was the purpose of the helps ministry?

DAY FOUR: NOT EVERYONE IS
CALLED TO BE AN APOSTLE, PROPHET,
TEACHER, EVANGELIST, OR PASTOR

When God calls people to work for Him, they usually assume He wants them to preach. However, God also calls people to sweep floors or work in the nursery.

Read 1 Corinthians 12:14-28. In those verses, the analogy used by the apostle Paul to explain the body of Christ was that of the human body. If one part is missing or malfunctioning, the body suffers loss and is handicapped.

God knew it would take many different ministries to keep a church family strong and healthy. If one failed, the others would suffer for it.

Another thing that is important to remember is that God sets each member where He wills, not where the member wills. God knows where you will be the most effective in caring for His people. When every part does its job, there is no division in the church body. You may not be the pastor, but God will give you a similar vision.

You can share in the effort to achieve that goal and share in the reward for helping the pastor accomplish God's commission. The helps ministry is a sort of apprenticeship program. When you prove yourself faithful and obedient in one job, God will promote you to another.

DAY FOUR STUDY QUESTIONS

1. Who decides what job you will do in the church?
2. Why does God set members in the church as He wills?
3. What happens when all members do their parts (1 Cor. 12:25)?
4. How does 1 Corinthians 12:14-28 apply to your church? What do those verses say to you?
5. What happens to those who share in the effort to bring to pass the pastor's God-given vision?
6. What would happen if everyone in your church decided to become a preacher?

DAY FIVE: THE DISCIPLES HAD HELPS MINISTRIES

The best example of helps ministries in the Bible can be seen in the events of Jesus' life. He came to earth to live a natural life before God in such a way that we could imitate and follow it. Look at a few experiences Jesus had:

In Matthew 10:5-8, Jesus sent out the twelve disciples. Why did He not go Himself?

Like any other shepherd, Jesus was only one man. He could do only so much by Himself. God gave Him the ministry of helps to expand His ability to minister to the people in all of the towns and villages to which He went.

In Matthew 14:15-21, we read about Jesus multiplying the loaves and fishes to feed more than 5,000 people. How was the food distributed? He did it through the ministry of helps, just as any pastor today would have to do.

In Matthew 8:23-26, Jesus was asleep in the boat during a storm at sea that threatened to sink them. How could anyone sleep through a storm like that? Sleeping through a storm is easy when you are physically exhausted from preaching. The disciples were doing the rowing so that Jesus could get the rest He so badly needed.

Maybe this is a good reason for you to help your pastor. When the disciples got into trouble during the storm, Jesus was there to take charge and rebuke the storm. Your pastor will do the same for you, if you give him the chance to be the leader and shepherd. But he can only do this if you give him time to rest by doing the jobs he otherwise would have to do.

The ministry of helps also handled the Last Supper for Jesus. Read Mark 14:12-16.

Jesus made great use of the ministry of helps in His time. God's men and women today have the same problems handling everything that needs to be done that Moses and Jesus did. God wants to make the same use of the ministry of helps today that He did in times past.

DAY FIVE STUDY QUESTIONS

1. In Matthew 10:5-8, why did Jesus send out the disciples instead of going Himself?
2. How did Jesus manage to distribute food to the 5,000 in Matthew 14:15-21?
3. In Matthew 8:23-26, there is another reason why Jesus needed the ministry of helps. What is it?
4. Who made the preparations for the Last Supper?
5. If you were to help your pastor as the disciples helped Jesus, what would happen in your church?

19

WEEK TWO:
THE WORK OF THE
MINISTRY OF HELPS

DAY ONE: THE STRONG CHURCH

But now hath God set the members every one of them in the body, as it hath pleased him.

And whether one member suffer, all the members suffer with it; or one member be honoured, all the members rejoice with it.

Now ye are the body of Christ, and members in particular.

And God hath set some in the church, first apostles, secondarily prophets, thirdly teachers, after that miracles, then gifts of healings, helps, governments, diversities of tongues.

1 Corinthians 12:18,26-28

The ministry of helps is a supernatural ministry set in a church by God to help bring to pass the vision or goal God gave the pastor. The simple definition of helps is "one who gives assistance to the weak and needy."

In verse 18, we see that every member is put in the church for a purpose. Every believer has a job to do in helping to care for God's people.

Verse 25 says, "but that the members should have the same care one for another." Caring for someone is not a mental attitude but an action whereby you watch out for the needs and welfare of others.

In verse 26, you can see that when you do not do your part, someone else suffers. When people are suffering, you should be there to comfort them. When they rejoice, you should be there to rejoice with them and spur them on. (Heb. 10:24.)

God never intended for any believer to be a pew sitter week after week. He put you in your church to help. Where people do not help, the body of Christ is weak.

Your church is made stronger when you are strong in the ministry of helps toward others. The church is weak when everyone looks at a problem and says, "I wish someone would do something about that."

You are that someone set in the church by God to do something about it!

DAY ONE STUDY QUESTIONS

1. What kind of ministry is the helps ministry?

2. Why was the helps ministry set in the church?

3. How many members are set in the church by God (1 Cor. 12:18)?

4. How are you to minister to your brethren (1 Cor. 12:25)?

5. What happens to the church if you do not do your part?

6. What makes the body of Christ weak?

DAY TWO: ORDER OF AUTHORITY
AND GOD'S ANOINTING

Read Numbers 11:10-17, which I wrote about earlier in these lessons. Moses was placed by God to oversee and care for His people, the Israelites. He was anointed to do the job and had God's ability to lead the people for the Lord.

As you see from those verses, a time came when the job was too big for one man. So God set the ministry of helps in the nation to assist Moses in caring for the people. Seventy elders were supernaturally empowered to assist and help Moses, the man with the vision. These men then also had the vision for what Moses was doing and had the same heart to get it done.

The anointing of God came down through a definite order. God's anointing went to Moses; Moses' anointing flowed to the seventy called to help. God has the same order today. He gave all power to Jesus, who sent the Holy Spirit, who called and anointed the five-fold ministry. (Eph. 4:11.)

Where does the anointing go from there? To you! You are the one those men and women of God are to equip and perfect. (Eph. 4:12.)

Your pastor is sent by God to train you to work building up Christ's body, the church. The pastor does not build up the church. He is supposed to train you to do it. Listen and learn from him so God can use you in your own ministry. The pastor's vision and anointing will flow into you if you will let it.

God will enable you to do the job just as He did Moses' men and Jesus' disciples.

DAY TWO STUDY QUESTIONS

1. What was Moses anointed to do?
2. What did God do when the job became too big for Moses alone?
3. Whose anointing did the seventy receive?
4. What were they supernaturally empowered to do?
5. In addition to the anointing, what else did those seventy elders share with Moses?
6. What is your pastor sent by God to do in the church?
7. What is your job in the church (Eph. 4:12)?

DAY THREE: SERVING GOD'S CHOSEN MAN

In Exodus 24:13, God's chosen man had a minister. Joshua was called to minister to Moses. The word *minister* in that context does not mean *preacher* but *servant*.

In a restaurant, the job of a waitress is to "minister" to you, to serve your table. Whatever your need is for that meal, she is to make sure it is met. What kind of waitress would she be if she never were around when you needed something? A good waitress watches carefully over your table and is there whenever you need her.

Joshua was chosen by God to wait on, or to serve, Moses. He was to help Moses by serving his needs so that Moses could keep his mind on God's work.

Joshua was the only one allowed to go with Moses to Mount Sinai and see the spectacular things of God that Moses saw. Why? Joshua was allowed to be involved at such a momentous time because he was a faithful servant to God's chosen man.

Being a servant was a menial thing to most people—and still is considered that way—but Joshua saw it as a ministry unto the Lord. Eventually, he was promoted to the position of leader of all Israel!

Your pastor will be more effective if he is not concerned with day-to-day duties such as sweeping the floor, mowing the lawn, or painting the church. The list is endless, and it puts an endless load on the pastor who does not have someone to help him or her.

I would rather have my pastor before God in prayer and in the Word than have him sweeping the floor. I want him perfectly in tune with God so that he can minister to the people. In Acts 6:2-3, the apostles realized this:

> Then the twelve called the multitude of the disciples unto them, and said, It is not reason that we should leave the word of God, and serve tables.
>
> Wherefore, brethren, look ye out among you seven men of honest report, full of the Holy Ghost and wisdom, whom we may appoint over this business.

DAY THREE STUDY QUESTIONS

1. Who did God give Moses to help him?

2. What does the word *minister* mean?

3. How is a person who serves his pastor like a witness?

4. Why did God give Moses a man to serve him?

5. How will it help your pastor if you serve him as Joshua did Moses?

6. In Acts 6:2, what did the apostles say was their primary duty?

7. What benefits did Joshua derive from faithfully serving God's chosen man?

DAY FOUR: ELISHA, THE FAITHFUL MINISTER

In 2 Kings 2:1-15, we are told of Elijah the prophet, as he came to the end of his ministry. God was preparing to take him home. When Elijah was gone, God would need someone else to carry on. Elisha was the man chosen by God for the job.

There are three things to notice about Elisha:

1. He served Elijah for a number of years.

2. He was faithful to the man with the vision.

3. He eventually was promoted.

Ten years is a long time to be following someone around, acting as his servant. But God knew what He was doing. Those years are what it took to mold and shape Elisha by experience into the kind of man God needed.

You may be thinking, *I have been here five years, and I am still a Sunday school teacher. When is God going to promote me?*

God will promote you when He knows you are ready to be promoted.

Just as Elisha was faithful to the man with the vision, you must prove yourself faithful to the man with the vision under whom God has set you.

Elisha not only was promoted in the end, but he received a double-portion of Elijah's anointing. He did twice as many miracles as Elijah.

Do not "put God in a box" regarding how long you serve a man of God. If you are faithful, God will promote you when He is ready and when you are ready.

DAY FOUR STUDY QUESTIONS

1. How long did Elisha serve Elijah?
2. Why did the Lord have Elisha serve Elijah for so long?
3. When does God promote someone?
4. How do you prove your faithfulness to God and man?
5. What did Elisha receive for his faithful service to Elijah?

DAY FIVE: THE FRUIT OF A FAITHFUL SERVANT

You may think you are not qualified for the ministry of helps. However, you need to remember that it is God who qualifies a person for a place of service in the body of Christ. This qualifying is the supernatural part of the ministry of helps.

What then is the natural side, or your part in the helps ministry?

The one thing only you can supply to your ministry is faithfulness. God cannot make you faithful to His will and plan for your life. You must decide to be faithful and trustworthy. This is the main element you must bring into your ministry to God and to the church.

The Bible has much to say about those who are faithful:

• In Proverbs 13:17, the faithful enjoy health. God blesses them with health and happiness because of their obedience.

• In Proverbs 25:13, a faithful servant is said to refresh his master. How would you like to be a blessing and a refreshing to your pastor? That is what God said a faithful servant would do.

• In Proverbs 28:20, God promises that the faithful servant will abound with blessings. Good things will come his way. When you set your mind to see after your pastor's welfare, God will take care of yours.

• In Daniel 6:4, we see the testimony of the faithful servant. No fault or wrong can be found in him. There is nothing he can be accused of because he is right with God. Faithfulness will put you in a place of honor in the eyes of your pastor.

DAY FIVE STUDY QUESTIONS

1. Who qualifies you for the ministry of helps?
2. What important ingredient can only you bring to the ministry of helps?
3. What belongs to the faithful (Prov. 13:17)?
4. What is another characteristic of a faithful servant (Prov. 14:5)?
5. What effect does the faithful servant have on the one he serves?
6. What will you abound in if you are faithful (Prov. 28:20)?

20

WEEK THREE:
HAVING A VISION

DAY ONE: YOU MUST HAVE A VISION

If any of you lack wisdom, let him ask of God, that giveth to all men liberally, and upbraideth not; and it shall be given him.

But let him ask in faith, nothing wavering. For he that wavereth is like a wave of the sea driven with the wind and tossed.

For let not that man think that he shall receive any thing of the Lord.

A double minded man is unstable in all his ways.

James 1:5-8

*D*ouble minded means you do not stick to one way of thinking. In the helps ministry, it refers to an individual who has received direction from God but keeps getting off track.

If God has called you to help the pastor by being an usher, do not try to fill some other position. Wisdom from God belongs to the single-minded Christian who sticks to what God has given him until it is done. We must resist the temptation to get our fingers into other things.

God has given your pastor a vision for your church, and he is responsible to bring it to pass. However, he will need help. That is why God has placed you there: to be a minister of helps to your pastor so that the vision can be reached.

A vision is a goal and a direction from God, a divine guidance that God gives you. Put faith with corresponding action to bring it to pass.

Proverbs 29:18 says:

> **Where there is no vision, the people perish: but he that keepeth the law, happy is he.**

Christians without a vision die. They shrivel up like fruit that has been on the tree too long. Those who will receive, and act on, the part of the pastor's vision which God gives them to perform will experience the supernatural working of God in their lives.

DAY ONE STUDY QUESTIONS

1. What does it mean to be "double minded" in your calling from God?

2. What does James 1:7 say the double-minded person receives from God?

3. What are you to be for your pastor? Why has God put you

in his church?

4. What does Proverbs 29:18 say about people without a
    vision?

5. What happens to those who act on the part of the pastor's
    vision which God has given them?

6. How do you protect the vision God has given you
    (Hab. 2:2,3)?

7. Why should you write down what God has told you to do
    in the church?

DAY TWO: GOD GIVES THE VISION

**(As it is written, I have made thee a father of many nations,)
before him whom he believed, even God, who quickeneth the dead,
and calleth those things which be not as though they were.**

Romans 4:17

You can see that it was God who gave Abraham the vision of
becoming the father of many nations. Romans 4:18 calls that vision
hope. When all hope of having a son was gone, God gave Abraham
supernatural hope. On the other hand, another name for supernatural
hope is *vision*. God showed Abraham what things would come to
pass if he cooperated.

The Lord also has given your pastor hope, or a vision, for the
future. There are four ways God gives people this kind of vision:

First, He could speak to your heart.

Second, He could give you an open vision—one you could see with your eyes.

Third, He might give you an inward vision.

Fourth, He might show you that vision in His Word.

Those who are called to the ministry of helps will have the same vision from God as the pastor. You may not get the vision the same way your pastor did, but God will put His vision in you as He sees fit.

Abraham received the fulfillment of his vision because he had faith in God's ability and willingness to do it. Paul tells us that we also must walk by faith and not by sight. (2 Cor. 5:7.) If we are faithful, God will bring that vision to pass; so have faith in the fulfillment of your vision.

In Proverbs 29:18, God said that people perish (fail) without a vision. Your church will fail without a vision on which you can put your faith.

Hebrews 11:1 says that faith gives substance (reality or existence) to things hoped for. If you have no hope or vision, then you have nothing to trust and believe God for; therefore, nothing will happen or come to pass in your life or the church.

God is in the hope-giving business, so when He speaks to you, listen to Him!

DAY TWO STUDY QUESTIONS

1. What vision did God give Abraham that exercised his faith?

2. What is another name for supernatural hope?

3. What are the four kinds of visions God gives?

4. Why would God give you the same vision as your pastor?

5. What did Abraham have to do to receive the fulfillment of the vision God gave him?

6. What causes people to fail (Prov. 29:18)?

7. What does faith bring to pass (Heb. 11:1)?

DAY THREE: HELPING GOD'S MAN WITH THE VISION

And it came to pass, when Moses held up his hand, that Israel prevailed: and when he let down his hand, Amalek prevailed.

But Moses' hands were heavy; and they took a stone, and put it under him, and he sat thereon; and Aaron and Hur stayed up his hands, the one on the one side, and the other on the other side; and his hands were steady until the going down of the sun.

Exodus 17:11,12

We can see the part that Moses' helpers played in overcoming Amalek. God told Moses how to win the battle, and Aaron and Hur helped. They did not win it, but they helped Moses win it.

God will always send people with the man of vision. If you want to be where things are happening in the Lord, join yourself to the man God sends you to and help him work toward the fulfillment of his vision.

God's will for your church is expressed in the vision or goal He has given to your pastor. Like Moses, your pastor will encounter times when he needs support to continue in the way the Lord has directed. Do not run ahead of him when he appears to be going too slow.

Sometimes we are quick to criticize a pastor for the way he is handling something. We need to remember that he is the man with the vision, the one God called to do it. Support your pastor's arms in the warfare with the enemy. See the supernatural move of the Lord.

You can be one who takes part in bringing about God's purpose in the land if only you will learn to be like Aaron and Hur—simply content to hold up the arms of the man of vision, knowing he cannot make it unless you, or someone like you, holds up his arms.

DAY THREE STUDY QUESTIONS

1. What part did Moses' helpers play in the battle with Amalek?
2. Who did God tell how to win the battle?
3. When God gives a man a vision, what else does He give him to carry it out?
4. How does God reveal His will, or goal, for your church?
5. Why should you be careful not to criticize or run ahead of your pastor in God's work?

DAY FOUR: BEING KNIT TOGETHER

So all the men of Israel were gathered against the city, knit together as one man.

Judges 20:11

They were organized so that each man supported and protected the other. No man would fight alone, but rather with the combined force of the entire nation.

The church has been called by God to be knit together as one body. Our success in this world depends on unity! The best way to beat an army is to scatter its soldiers—stop the unity! Satan wants to do that to your church. We are workers together with God. (1 Cor. 3:9.)

If you want to work with the Holy Spirit, you will have to work together with your brothers in the Lord, because that is who He is working with.

Now I beseech you, brethren, by the name of our Lord Jesus Christ, that ye all speak the same thing, and that there be no divisions among you; but that ye be perfectly joined together in the same mind and in the same judgment.

1 Corinthians 1:10

God's idea of unity includes everyone speaking the same thing with no divisions — one in mind and opinion. These qualities produce one thing, shown in Genesis 11:1-6. God Himself said nothing would be impossible for the body of people that built the

Tower of Babel. Why? He said that because of their unity. That is why He changed the one language of the world into many — to break up the unity of minds.

Jesus said in Matthew 18:19:

> **Again I say unto you, That if two of you shall agree on earth as touching any thing that they shall ask, it shall be done for them of my Father which is in heaven.**

> **God will work and move supernaturally among His people when they are in harmony together.**

DAY FOUR STUDY QUESTIONS

1. In your own words, write down what it means to be "knit together as one man."

2. On what does the success of the church in this world depend?

3. What is the best way to beat an army?

4. What is Satan trying to do to God's army?

5. Who will God work with (1 Cor. 3:9)?

6. Why must you work together with your brothers in the Lord?

7. What elements are included in God's idea of unity (1 Cor. 1:10)?

DAY FIVE: THE HELPS MINISTRY
IN THE EARLY CHURCH

In Acts 6:1-7, you will see that the early church had a ministry of helps that greatly aided the growth of Christianity in the world. There are seven things you need to notice about this event:

1. The Word of God increased (spread) after the ministry of helps was added to the church.

2. Those in the helps ministry had hands laid upon them to receive the anointing to do the job.

3. The purpose was to give the men with the vision time for Bible study and prayer.

4. Stephen did mighty miracles because he had proven himself faithful in serving; therefore, he was promoted by God to the miracle ministry.

5. Church growth resulted from the work of the helps ministry.

6. This demonstrates that God will add to your church as well when He knows that you can care for them.

7. The people did not lay hands on those called, but the apostles did, as Christ's direct representatives of His authority on earth.

All of these things combined to produce a supernatural, growing church that turned the world upside down. There is no reason we cannot do that again—if we learn from the experiences of those who made up the first-generation church.

DAY FIVE STUDY QUESTIONS

1. What aided the growth of the early church?

2. Who did God appoint to lay hands on the ministry of helps?

3. Why did the Word of God increase?

4. Why did Stephen get promoted to a miracle-working minister?

5. Why did God set the ministry of helps in the church?

6. How did God equip the seven men for the ministry of helps?

PRAYER OF SALVATION

God loves you—no matter who you are, no matter what your past. God loves you so much that He gave His one and only begotten Son for you. The Bible tells us that "...whoever believes in him shall not perish but have eternal life" (John 3:16 NIV). Jesus laid down His life and rose again so that we could spend eternity with Him in heaven and experience His absolute best on earth. If you would like to receive Jesus into your life, say the following prayer out loud and mean it from your heart.

Heavenly Father, I come to You admitting that I am a sinner. Right now, I choose to turn away from sin, and I ask You to cleanse me of all unrighteousness. I believe that Your Son, Jesus, died on the cross to take away my sins. I also believe that He rose again from the dead so that I might be forgiven of my sins and made righteous through faith in Him. I call upon the name of Jesus Christ to be the Savior and Lord of my life. Jesus, I choose to follow You and ask that You fill me with the power of the Holy Spirit. I declare that right now I am a child of God. I am free from sin and full of the right-eousness of God. I am saved in Jesus' name. Amen.

If you prayed this prayer to receive Jesus Christ as your Savior for the first time, please contact us on the Web at **www.harrisonhouse.com** to receive a free book.

Or you may write to us at

Harrison House • P.O. Box 35035 • Tulsa, Oklahoma 74153

ABOUT THE AUTHOR

Buddy Bell has been serving pastors and families in the local church since1977.

In 1986, he founded Ministry of Helps International in Tulsa, Oklahoma where he serves as president.

Dr. Bell is also an international teacher and succesful author.

To contact him:

Ministry of Helps International
P.O. Box 1709
Sand Springs, OK 74063
email:help@mohi.org
www.mohi.org